Peaceful
Dwelling

Peaceful Dwelling

MEDITATIONS FOR HEALING AND LIVING

Madeline Ko-i Bastis

Tuttle Publishing
BOSTON · RUTLAND, VERMONT · TOKYO

First published in 2000 by Tuttle Publishing, an imprint of Periplus Editions (HK) Ltd., with editorial offices at 153 Milk Street, Boston, Massachusetts, 02109.

Cover photographs © Horace Bristol/Corbis

page 1	From *Tao Te Ching by Lao Tzu, a New English Version, with Foreword and Notes by Stephen Mitchell* © 1988 by Stephen Mitchell. Reprinted with permission by HarperCollins Publishers, New York
page 17	Exerpted from *The Tao of Healing* by Haven Treviño © 1993. Reprinted with permission of New World Library, Novato, CA 94949, www.nwlib.com
page 18	*Blooming Of A Lotus* by Thich Nhat Hanh © 1993 by Thich Nhat Hanh Reprinted by permission of Beacon Press, Boston
page 91	From *One Robe, One Bowl—the Zen Poetry of Ryokan* translated by John Stevens © 1977. Reprinted by permission of Weatherhill Publishing
page 113	From *One Hundred Butterflies* by Peter Levitt © Peter Levitt Reprinted by permission of the author

Library of Congress Cataloging-in-Publication Data
Bastis, Madeline Ko-i.
    Peaceful dwelling : meditations for healing & living / Madeline Ko-i Bastis.— 1st ed.
       p. cm.
    Includes bibliographical references.
    ISBN: 0-8048-3234-X (pbk.)
       1. Spiritual life—Buddhism. 2. Health—Religious aspects—Buddhism. 3. Compassion (Buddhism) 4. Peace—Religious aspects—Buddhism.
    BQ4302 .B39 2001
    294.3'4435—dc21   00-032594

Distributed by

North America
Tuttle Publishing
Distribution Center
Airport Industrial Park
364 Innovation Drive
North Clarendon, VT 05759-9436
Tel: (802) 773-8930
Tel: (800) 526-2778
Fax: (802) 773-6993

Asia Pacific
Berkeley Books Pte Ltd
5 Little Road #08-01
Singapore 536983
Tel: (65) 280-1330
Fax: (65) 280-6290

Japan
Tuttle Publishing
RK Building, 2nd Floor
2-13-10 Shimo-Meguro, Meguro-Ku
Tokyo 153 0064
Tel: (03) 5437-0171
Tel: (03) 5437-0755

05 04 03 02 01 00   9 8 7 6 5 4 3 2 1

Printed in the United States of America

To study the Buddha Way is to study the Self
To study the Self is to forget the Self
To forget the Self is to be enlightened by the 10,000 things.

—Zen Master Dōgen

This book is dedicated to the 10,000 teachers I met during my chaplaincy training, especially Roshi Peter Muryo Matthiessen, Chaplain Mary Jean Metzger, and all my patients.

Thank you for illuminating my life.

Contents

───────────

THREE
BEING PRESENT:
MINDFULNESS OF BREATHING 17

───────────

FOUR
MOVING MEDITATION:
MINDFULNESS IN EVERYDAY LIFE 43

───────────

FIVE
OPENING THE HEART:
METTA (LOVING-KINDNESS) PRACTICES 67

Contents

───────────

Contents

Acknowledgments

I would like to thank all those who helped make this book possible:

Peggy Block for believing I had something to say and Barbara Wersba who believed that I could say it.

All the teachers who introduced me to the meditation practices found in this book, especially Stephen Smith and Dr. Richard Boerstler.

Jan Johnson of Tuttle who rescued my proposal from the slush pile, suggested the final structure, and offered encouragement throughout the entire publishing process; Caroline Pincus whose careful reading and advice helped clarify and simplify the text; Jane Merryman who copyedited the final manuscript.

To the patients whose stories make the book come alive and the workshop participants who asked the questions that challenged me to deepen my own meditation practice.

I dedicate this book to you.

May your hearts be filled with peace.

Like many people, I began my meditation practice when I didn't know what else to do.

For me the low point came after I had been sober for a year. Physically I was fine, but there was a spiritual and emotional emptiness in my life—a longing in my heart for healing.

Years ago, I was celebrating my birthday with my sister in a local restaurant. We ordered a bottle of wine and each of us had a glass. That was all she had, just one! How was she able to be satisfied with a mere sip when I craved the entire bottle? I took a second glass, promising myself that I wouldn't take another. I could not *not* drink, and before dessert the bottle was empty.

For the first time, I became drunk in front of another person. The facade was shattered and I admitted that I was an alcoholic, just like my father and grandfather. I was ready to surrender and seek help.

I attended recovery meetings, but after a year of sobriety with no alcohol to assuage them, my anger, depression, dread, and an inner emptiness flared and I was suffering.

I then enrolled in a twenty-five-dollar, three-session meditation class at a local high school. During the first few minutes that first night, I noticed a slight shift in my consciousness and afterwards I felt calmer, more like the person I wanted to be. That's all it took.

Meditation immediately made me feel better. Focusing on my breath helped my chattering mind settle down. I didn't have to control anything; all I had to do was watch my breath. What a relief to be able to sit quietly without thinking about the past or planning the future.

I began to sit in meditation every day at home, first for ten minutes, then for longer periods of time. Even on days when my thoughts were whirling like a dervish, I felt better after having meditated.

My physical energy soared, I slept more soundly, and I seemed more able to concentrate on work. After I found my first teacher and began to attend a local *zendo* (Zen meditation place), my meditation practice became an integral part of my life.

During the many retreats I attended, my mind became a still pool and insights about my life surfaced. It was a time to face the traits and habits, what Buddhist teachers call conditioning, that created suffering for myself and others. As I sat in meditation, annoyance would arise—the room was too hot or too cold; the person next to me was breathing too loudly; I had to wait in line too long to see the teacher. Annoyance blossomed into anger and I began to understand that it was the underlying motif of my life. Because I was in a monastery setting, I couldn't just get up and leave. I learned to sit in the midst of my suffering, feeling my feelings. Eventually they dissipated. Other emotions and memories also arose, and I learned to sit with them. How empowering to be able to face my suffering without denial or taking a drink!

Eventually, I began to experience real joy in my daily life. No longer did everyday tasks like doing laundry, cleaning the house, or washing dishes seem tedious and pointless. A sense of humor emerged, and I began to feel gratitude for the gift of my life. When the car broke down or a water pipe burst, I no longer flew off the handle; I just did what needed to be done. Drama disappeared from my life and was replaced by serenity.

Slowly but surely the inner judging voice that whispered that I was not good enough, not perfect enough, evaporated and I was able to accept and embrace all parts of myself, the good and the not so good. I began to feel connected to the people around me and to my surroundings as well. As I came to appreciate myself, I came to appreciate other people, and my relationships improved. Spiritual and emotional healing had begun.

After several years of Zen meditation and study, I felt a need to bring my practice into the world. In 1993, inspired by a vision quest and by my father's death, I entered a three-year training program to become a hospital chaplain. I wanted to learn how to care for dying people, especially AIDS and cancer patients, and teach them meditation.

Two years passed before I was asked to teach meditation in the hospital. It didn't happen according to my schedule; the invitation came only when I was ready. First, I needed to learn how to be present for my patients' suffering without being overwhelmed with grief or closing myself off from their pain. I had to learn to sit quietly and listen, just as I sat during meditation and watched my thoughts arise and pass away. I had to bring the same quality of attention to a teenager with tonsillitis as to a dying person, and to minister to doctors and nurses on the staff as well as distraught family members. I had to learn that each of us deserves healing.

At first I led weekly loving-kindness meditation groups in detox and the psychiatric ward and for the AIDS staff and outpatients with AIDS. Occasionally I meditated with individual patients.

In 1996, after being certified as the first Buddhist hospital chaplain and ordained as a Zen priest, I founded Peaceful Dwelling Project with the idea that I wanted to make Buddhist healing meditations available to everyone, no matter what their faith tradition.

Initially, we served cancer and AIDS patients, the dying, and professional caregivers in danger of burnout. Peaceful Dwelling's mission expanded to include visiting a shelter for homeless men with AIDS, a day-care center for emotionally disadvantaged adults, a residence for battered women, addicted inmates in a county jail, a senior citizens' center, a kindergarten class, and women's support groups.

Members of the local community began to seek help: a teacher overcome by stress, a woman going through a difficult divorce, a man on the verge of retirement, a parent with an autistic child.

Because we work with a wide spectrum of people, the meditation practices have evolved to suit the needs of each individual or group. In this book I'll share some of these practices with you.

Although the stories I tell come mainly from my work with people who are physically ill, they apply to everyone. For, meditation does not treat physical symptoms; it reaches to the roots of suffering. In the quiet space brought about by meditation, our anger, fear, sadness, desire, and delusions are revealed.

Meditation brings the serenity that enables us to look at our deepest hurts and to embrace them, as a mother embraces her child.

We begin to trust that we can heal ourselves. All we have to do is sit down and begin to follow our breath.

One

Meditation

A PATH TO HEALING

She who is centered in the Way
can go where she wishes without danger.
She perceives the universal harmony
even amid great pain, because she has found
peace in her heart.

TAO TE CHING, STEPHEN MITCHELL, TRANSLATOR

Thom was the first patient I met who had a meditation practice. He lived in a rickety migrant worker's shack on the north fork of Long Island. The single room was crammed with a homemade Murphy bed, and the bathroom lacked the one luxury that Thom coveted—a tub.

The glass in the sliding door was cracked and cloudy, patched with plastic sheeting. But through that door! Sunlight and space and riotous color: luminous red competed with purple and chartreuse, golden yellow contrasted with burgundy, clear cobalt muted burning orange. The air was a medley of odors: phlox, lavender, cleome, manure drying in the sun. The calls of grackles, robins, and mockingbirds blended in the breeze. Soft, gray lamb's ears nestled beneath heavily thorned old roses; silver lace vine festooned rugged native cedar; and everywhere lilies poked up amid wild strawberries and jimsonweed.

Thom didn't discriminate among flowers—he prized wild goldenrod and chicory as much as he did his antique roses and Dutch bulbs. Thom's garden was quirky. He had never liked formulas or regulations in his work as a fine artist, in his lifestyle, or in his garden. When someone told him that short plants should be planted in front of taller ones, or that flowers of the same variety should be massed together for effect, he'd scoff, "Who made that rule?"

It was in his garden that Thom meditated. He told me that one day when he was sitting with his legs on a stool, he felt the wind rush in through the soles of his feet and blow his entire being out of his body. He felt cleaned out and light and free, and filled with immeasurable joy.

After this experience Thom softened. Anger toward the lover who had abandoned him when he was diagnosed with AIDS evaporated, and a door opened in the wall he had erected to separate himself from others. Thom left his garden to reveal his AIDS to the community, visiting schools to encourage kids to protect themselves from the virus. He worked an AIDS hotline and although he lived on disability, he anonymously helped support an AIDS patient who was worse off than he was.

Thom had been healed by his meditation practice. Sitting quietly in his garden following his breath had opened a calm space. The wind that rushed through his soul banished his inner turmoil and left the gift of peace in his heart. During the last months of his illness, Thom retreated to his garden, this time with many friends. They planted tulips and hyacinths and roses.

In Thom's words, "The tulips will bloom or not; it doesn't matter if I'm here—life will go on as it should. But what fun to dig in the earth and plant the future!" Thom did see the tulips bloom, but soon after, he died in the hospital of kidney failure.

I had visited Thom over a period of eighteen months and witnessed the blooming of his soul and was present on the last day of his life. The June memorial service was held in his garden among the budding roses and Thom's ashes were scattered in the tiny paradise.

Later, Thom's closest friend suggested that I go to the garden to dig up some plants since there was no one to care for them. I put it off—I sprained my ankle; it was too hot; I didn't have time. Perhaps I wasn't ready to face Thom's absence from my life. Finally, on the last day of summer I drove to the garden.

I was devastated. The summer drought had killed everything. The garden was no more than an overgrown vacant lot, filled with dry tendrils and dusty leaves in shades of tan and gray and umber. No color, no sound, no taste, no touch, no life. Like Thom, the garden had turned to dust. In the far reaches of the former Eden, hidden by weeds, was a chair Thom had made from scraps of decking. It was as quirky and asymmetrical and interesting as Thom.

I've placed it near my own pond and I can see the empty chair through my window. It doesn't really seem empty and sometimes I can imagine Thom sitting there with the wind blowing through the soles of his feet.

Thom faced the end of his life with equanimity, surrounded by friends. His demons were released and he allowed himself to love and be loved by others. Was he healed? I believe he would say yes.

Often people don't begin to meditate until there is a disruption in their lives. When everything is going well, there doesn't seem to be a reason to meditate. We all have busy schedules and it's difficult to make time.

Generally, it takes suffering to motivate us to begin. The suffering can be caused by external forces: contracting an illness, loss of a job, the death of a dear friend, a drop in the stock market. Or it can be internal: addiction, lack of self-esteem, loneliness, fear. Sometimes it is a yearning deep inside to understand the meaning of our life. No matter how or where the suffering arises, meditation can bring us to a clear place where we know that all is well. Like Thom.

When we meditate, each of us enters the same path that the Buddha walked twenty-five hundred years ago. When he was confronted with sickness, old age, and death, he determined to find the way to end suffering. He practiced and found the answer, and so can we.

Understanding Suffering

When we say that meditation can relieve suffering, it is important to understand what we mean by suffering. We tend to think that pain and suffering are the same, but they are not. Pain is the body's way of alerting us to an imbalance or injury: If you break your leg, it hurts.

Suffering, on the other hand, is caused by our *relationship* to pain. The effort of fighting the pain contracts the body and causes additional pain. We may replay the incident over and over again, wondering how we could have avoided the broken leg: If only I had paid more attention; if only someone had fixed that rickety porch step; if only I had stayed in bed; if only . . . the accident wouldn't have happened. Then we may worry about the future—how long will I be laid up, will the pain get worse, will I still be able to play tennis? Invariably the question "why me?" surfaces and along with it, anger, resentment, and impatience. We have created our own suffering.

How much simpler it would be if we could pay attention to the sensation alone. One day, after teaching a grueling weekend workshop, I had to drive into Manhattan. I was tired but also wired from residual excitement, and as I turned onto the main road, I hit a tree. The front of the car crumpled, the air bags deployed, and a huge bump appeared on my head. I had seen the car approach the tree and as we hit, I simply noted "tree." Years of meditation practice had kicked in. Instead of thinking: What was the damn tree doing there, maybe if I had left five minutes earlier or later . . . my beautiful car is totaled—I simply noticed "tree." When an ambulance came the technicians were amazed to see that my blood pressure was normal as was my heart rate.

Later, I took care of the insurance and hospital forms and said good-by to the car. Things are as they are. No suffering.

Attachment is another source of our suffering. When things are going well in our lives our tendency is to want them to stay that way indefinitely, and we may begin to worry that they'll change. We attach ourselves like an octopus to the way things are, fearing that we'll lose them and that we'll be lost along with them. That attachment causes suffering.

Wanting causes suffering. When our lives seem to be in the doldrums and nothing exciting is happening, we crave novelty.

Denial causes suffering. When something difficult crops up in our lives, we want it to disappear. We try to push it away by denying it, becoming angry, or medicating ourselves with sex, drugs, and rock and roll.

None of these things works for very long, however. Finally, we throw up our hands and surrender. This is the first step on the spiritual path.

The Benefits of Meditation

Clinical studies indicate that the deep, relaxed state brought about by meditation can lower blood pressure, slow the heart-beat, reduce stress, and improve sleep. Some physicians believe that meditation can boost our immune system. New research is being done about the healing effects of intercessory prayer and meditation when it is done for others.

Regular practice has a calming effect on our lives—we are less likely to react to outer disturbances in ways that are harmful to ourselves and others. But these physical benefits are bonuses. Real healing begins with the spirit. Meditation quiets the mind and brings us to a clear space where we feel connected to everyone and everything. We understand, through our own experience, that we *are* everyone and everything.

A long, long time ago, a wealthy king named Indra asked his magician to create the most wondrous thing in the world. Cost was not a factor. Of course, Indra wanted it right now, as quickly as possible. "Be patient," the magician said, "and I will bring you the universe."

The magician took his time and then presented Indra with a beautiful net that reached throughout all space and time. At the intersection of each knot was a many-faceted diamond that reflected every other diamond. The reflections reached infinity. They embraced the past, present, and future.

There was no separation—everything was included—the large, perfectly cut diamonds and the chipped, flawed diamonds; the blue-white diamonds and the yellow diamonds. Each diamond, no matter what its size or color or condition was necessary to hold the net together. Each was important individually and as part of the whole.

When we experience ourselves as part of Indra's net, we become free from fear. We are able to embrace what is happening in us and around us without pushing it away or wanting it to change. We rest in a state of equanimity. From this calm space, free of self-centered desire, we can act with wisdom and compassion. This is where healing and transformation begin.

Meditation practice teaches us to live our lives in the present moment and to know that it is perfect and complete exactly as it is. All we have to do is pay attention. All we have to do is awaken to the present moment. All we have to do is realize that we are perfect and complete exactly as we are. What a relief!

A Palette of Practices

During my years of chaplaincy training I met hundreds of patients. Initially, I was determined to give them hope and courage. I wanted them to get well. I wanted them to die peaceful deaths. I wanted to teach them meditation. In fact, I wanted them to change.

My struggle lasted for a long time as I wrestled with my need to have things go the way I thought they should. Finally, I was too exhausted to struggle and I gave up my need to control things. I was ready to sit silently and listen to what others needed. When patients asked for a drink of water, I brought it; when they wanted to pray, I prayed; when they wished to meditate, I taught them how.

While my own practice is and has for many years been Zen Buddhism, as I visited patients who were suffering spiritually, emotionally, and physically, I began to develop a palette of practices to suit their unique experiences and situations.

Some people had no experience with meditation and found it scary. "You tryin' to hypnotize me?" one suspicious patient asked. Others who had strong ties to their religions thought that meditating might dislodge their faith. Some were in so much physical or psychological pain that they needed verbal guiding.

And so I explored meditations from different traditions that could be used with a broad spectrum of patients. Sometimes I didn't have to look very far; sometimes they just plopped into my lap.

One day I was called to Memorial Sloan-Kettering Cancer Center because a woman patient there had requested a Buddhist chaplain. The patient, Laurie, was still in her twenties, had a flourishing writing career, and lived with a sweet young man. Then she developed breast cancer and her life was turned inside out. Several months of chemotherapy and radiation had not helped and now she was near death.

Laurie had no ties to religion but felt that the Buddhist philosophy fit her intuited beliefs. We talked of many things—how tired she was of trying to hang on to life by undergoing difficult treatments, her wish to let go, and the feeling of relief she found in the Buddhist teachings of impermanence and no-self.

Her fiancé had found a book by Thich Nhat Hanh, *The Blooming of a Lotus,* and together they practiced the guided meditations. Laurie found solace in them. She asked that I meditate with her and pointed to a book on the side table.

This was my first brush with guided meditation. Instead of focusing on my own practice, I focused on another person. I felt a bond develop between us. Because of her illness, Laurie did not have the energy to sustain concentration by herself. My voice and presence helped her to achieve serenity. It felt as if we were praying together. Meditation no longer seemed so self-absorbed.

Gradually, I encountered other Buddhist meditations that seemed to help people who were experiencing suffering. I had to let go of my opinions about how meditation should be done and I explored traditions beyond my spartan Japanese Zen practice.

I incorporated aspects of the Theravadan tradition of Southeast Asia, which teaches practices in a sequential way to arouse wisdom (insight meditation) and compassion (*metta* and *karuna*); I brought in elements from Tibetan meditations, which rely heavily on visualization (like *phowa* and co-meditation for the dying). In short, I used whatever seemed to work.

Over the years I have incorporated the following types of meditation into my work:

- ❖ mindfulness of breathing, which focuses on the breath to teach us that everything changes. It can also reduce stress, alleviate physical pain, and help us develop serenity.

- ❖ walking meditation, to extend mindfulness to include body awareness. Walking meditation helps us bring attention to our daily activities, whether they are pleasant, unpleasant, or neutral, thereby enriching our lives. Being mindful to the process of our daily lives moment after moment awakens joy. Monitoring an addiction, undergoing chemotherapy, or performing menial chores become an adventure.

- ❖ metta (loving-kindness), opening the heart to love and acceptance of oneself and others. Metta speaks to those with low self-esteem, those who cannot forgive, and caregivers who traditionally put their own needs last and burn out.

- ❖ *tonglen* (taking and sending), which teaches us to work with physical and emotional pain and suffering and lessens feelings of isolation.

- co-meditation, originally used to ease a person's death. Co-meditation also releases difficult emotions, relieves stress, and forges a connection between the guide and the recipient.

- phowa, traditionally a meditation for the dying or dead. It can assuage feelings of loss for the bereaved and can easily be adapted as a healing meditation for the ill.

This book introduces you to these meditations and visualizations. I include only those practices that I have used for myself and with others. (There are many Buddhist practices not discussed here.) If you have meditated before, some of the following meditations may seem familiar, although their purposes may be different. For example, co-meditation, where you meditate with and for someone else, is traditionally used at the moment of death, but I find it works just as well for healing and letting go of difficult emotions.

When I would visit Carrie, a client with lung cancer, we would usually practice metta (see Chapter Four), but on one particular day she was overcome by fear. Her chemotherapy had been going well, but a sonogram had revealed two additional spots on her lung and she was returning to the hospital the next day for further tests. This time she needed something special and I asked her to lie on the couch. I meditated with her, asking her to imagine the fear leaving her body with each exhalation and ending with a healing visualization (see Chapter Six). Her anxiety abated, and I had found a new tool to use with people in distress.

If you have not meditated before, and even if you have, we will start with basic meditation practices. Because the breath is the anchor for most of the meditations in this book, we begin with a chapter on mindfulness of breathing. Then we move on to walking meditation, which helps us bring mindfulness into our daily activities. Next we work with developing love and acceptance for ourselves and others (loving-kindness). Compassion practices (karuna and tonglen) are then explored, and finally we work with letting go of difficult emotions and easing into death.

How to Use This Book

All the meditations in this book can be done for yourself or others. I suggest that you read through the entire book, then go back and reread and practice the meditations that interest you. Feel free to change the words to make the practice your own.

If you work with people who are physically ill or in emotional distress and plan to use these practices, familiarize yourself with the meditations so you'll feel comfortable guiding them. Practice one meditation at a time in depth. After a while, add a new one to your repertoire until you are able to intuitively choose the appropriate meditation for each situation.

Each chapter focuses on a different kind of meditation. I include basic instructions, complete guided meditation text, and stories of how the meditations have been used with people in varied circumstances. These vignettes are included to encourage you to use the meditations often and to inspire you to create new opportunities for their application.

Although many of the stories star persons who are ill, the underlying emotions are the same for everyone. For example, it makes no difference what you're afraid of—dying, getting old, or losing your lover—fear is fear. During the course of our exploration of mindfulness and other techniques, we'll learn to detach from the stories that we weave around our emotions. We'll discover that anger is anger, sadness is sadness, and we'll learn to regard them (and ourselves) in a compassionate way.

To keep the instructions simple, I save information on expanding your practice for a section in each chapter called "Going Deeper." Its question-and-answer format, which is based on the questions most commonly asked by participants in my workshops, can help you quickly find the information you need.

Each chapter concludes with a section entitled "Making the Practice Your Own." Here you'll find exercises and suggestions for projects to help you adapt the practices and incorporate what you've learned into your daily life.

Two

The Basics

Practice is already enlightenment.

ZEN MASTER DŌGEN

Because this book offers meditations from several traditions, there are no *shoulds* or *musts* or *have to's*. I offer several ways of sitting, breathing, walking. Choose the one that's the most comfortable for you. If a particular meditation seems right for you and you wish to practice it in depth, I encourage you to read one of the books listed in the resource list at the end of the book, try to find a group near you that practices on a regular basis, or look for a workshop or retreat in the tradition that appeals to you.

There is no right way or wrong way to meditate. It's the intention that's important. Each time you notice your mind wandering and you return to your practice, you are meditating. You are planting the seeds of serenity.

■

GETTING STARTED

Let's begin with just a few basics.

Posture

Perhaps you have seen statues of the Buddha sitting cross-legged. This is the traditional way of sitting, but there are actually several meditation postures, and I encourage you to experiment to find one that you can maintain for thirty minutes.

I have never been able to sit in the full-lotus posture (both feet resting on the thighs), but for many years sat half-lotus with only one foot on my thigh. As I got older, I drifted to quarter-lotus, resting one foot on the calf of the other leg. Now I sit in *seiza*, a kneeling posture with a cushion under the buttocks to take some of the burden off the knees.

I must admit that I used to be pretty proud of my ability to sit for long periods of time without moving and tended to feel superior to people who had to sit on chairs. When I began to lead meditation groups at hospitals or adult day-care centers, only chairs were available, so I sat in one, too. Surprise, surprise! It worked just as well.

Try sitting cross-legged first. This position is very stable because the base of your body is a tripod (buttocks and both knees touching the mat). Since Westerners do not usually sit this way, after a while each time we take the cross-legged position, the body (like Pavlov's dog) knows that it's time to meditate. After months of practice, as soon as you hit the cushion you will enter the meditative state easily. If this position is not possible, try the kneeling posture seiza, with cushion under buttocks. A little discomfort is okay; it helps us concentrate and keeps us from nodding off.

If you already have knee or back problems or are ill, sit in a chair. The important thing is to sit on the front two-thirds of the seat, taking care that your back doesn't rest against the back of the chair. Place both feet flat on the floor. Although most of your weight will be on the buttocks, there is a strong sense of being rooted to the earth.

When you first sit down whether on a cushion or chair, gently move your shoulders and neck to loosen them. Your head will be straight, not leaning back, dropping to your chest, or lolling to the side. Imagine there is a book on top of your head. Tuck your chin in. This may sound rigid, but there is a relaxed alertness to this body posture. Your erect spine allows the breath to reach your abdomen and come back up easily. Slouching may cause your back to ache and certainly invites drowsiness.

I do not suggest that you meditate while lying down because of the likelihood that you will fall asleep. However, if you are not able to leave your bed because of illness, you can certainly still meditate. Lie flat on your back with your hands clasped loosely over your abdomen. If possible, remove the pillow from the back of your head so that your body is lying flat. Turning your toes slightly outward helps to loosen leg muscles. Try to meditate with your eyes slightly open to guard against falling asleep, (although if you are ill and feeling particularly anxious, falling asleep can be a good thing).

Hands

Keep your hands in a position comfortable for you. In the cosmic *mudra,* the back of the left hand rests on the right palm, while the tips of the thumbs touch each other lightly. Place both hands in your lap. This mudra helps us monitor our awareness—when you notice that your thumbs droop, you are probably getting sleepy and your attention wanders. When your thumbs are tightly pressed together, you are probably too tense.

If you like, you can simply fold your hands in your lap. Another position is to place both palms on your knees. Each meditation tradition has its own mudra. If you have already learned one, then stay with it.

Find hand and body positions that you can hold without moving. If your body is twitching, your mind will not be still.

Eyes

To open or not to open, that is the question! Some traditions teach us to keep our eyes open, others to close them. Generally, we are taught to open our eyes to keep from falling asleep or drifting into daydreams. I suggest that you start with your eyes closed and if you notice that you're sleepy, open them. Unfocus your eyes and gaze at the floor in front of you at a forty-five-degree angle.

Breath

Each tradition has different instructions for breathing. Most of the meditations in this book ask you to inhale and exhale through the nose. If it makes sense for you to exhale through your mouth, it will be indicated before the particular meditation.

Going Deeper

Here are the most common beginner questions and comments about meditation:

Why should I sit on the edge of the chair?

If you sit deep in a chair, you'll be tempted to lean against the back and eventually you'll find yourself slumping, with rounded shoulders and a curved spine—and sleepiness is sure to follow. When you sit on the front two-thirds of a chair, the muscles at the back of your thighs won't fall asleep.

Sometimes when I try to meditate, my mouth fills with saliva and I have to keep swallowing.

At times beginning meditators are nervous. You might worry that you're not doing it correctly or feel uneasy because you don't know what to expect. Before you begin, inhale through your nose, exhale through your mouth, and swallow all the saliva in your mouth. Then place the tip of your tongue on the roof of your mouth near your teeth. This should help.

For people who've been meditating for a long time, excess saliva can still happen. When we reach a deep level of concentration, body fluids are stirred up. Although saliva is one manifestation, others could be tears or a sweat brought about by intense body temperature. Try to stay with the sensations in the body.

I have several meditation tapes and they have music in the background, is that okay?

Buddhist meditations generally do not use music. Although music can be relaxing, it can also be a distraction. In this book we'll try to penetrate surface calm and find a place of inner serenity.

Here's a Zen story:

A monk asked his teacher, "What is enlightenment?"
The teacher responded, "When I eat, I eat. When I sleep, I sleep."

When you listen to music, really listen. When you meditate, give it your full attention.

What's the best time of day to meditate?

Traditionally, monks meditate early in the morning and before bedtime. Each person's body clock is different—some of us are morning people, others are night owls. Decide which category you fall into and structure your daily practice accordingly. If your schedule makes it impossible for you to follow your body clock, then grab any time available during the day.

Making the Practice Your Own

The following suggestions are meant to help you get in the habit of meditating—and in a way that makes the most sense for you.

- ❖ If possible, meditate in the same place (even a corner of a bedroom is fine), using the same chair or cushion.

- ❖ Meditate at the same time each day.

- ❖ Choose an item of clothing—a sweatshirt or shawl or jacket—and make this your meditation "robe." Wear it only for meditation and know that each time you put it on you are ready to practice.

- ❖ Take a meaningful poem or prayer or saying that reflects your spirituality and write it beautifully or typeset it on your computer. Keep it near your meditation place.

- ❖ Each time you sit down to meditate, bow to your cushion or chair to remind yourself that you are doing a spiritual practice.

- ❖ Experiment with meditating outdoors in a lovely setting.

Relax and enjoy the practice.

Three

Being Present

MINDFULNESS OF BREATHING

Quiet the mind
Be still
And watch the breath of God
Rise and fall
In all things.
Allow God's breath
To be your breath;
Allow God's nature
To be your nature.

HAVEN TREVINO, *THE TAO OF HEALING*

We tend to take the breath for granted. How many of us realize that when we breathe the entire universe breathes with us? Each breath contains the entire cosmos and all eternity. With each in-breath we are born, with each out-breath we die. The breath is our ballast. Turning our attention to it, we find our center. In almost all meditation practices the breath is the anchor. Beginning meditators learn to be "mindful" of the breath, carefully watching it rise and fall.

When we become anxious or fearful, the first thing that happens is that our breath and heartbeat become irregular and our blood pressure rises. I would often find this in my work as a chaplain. When I visited patients in the emergency room, one of the most helpful things I could do was simply to hold their hand and ask them to follow their breath. The following meditation, adapted from one of Vietnamese Buddhist master Thich Nhat Hanh's practices, takes less than three minutes but brings the racing mind to a halt and slows the breath. I recommend that you try this whenever you need to return to your center:

Guided Meditation

Breathing in I know I am breathing in.
Breathing out I know I am breathing out.
In; Out (silence for five breaths as you watch the
    inhalations and exhalations)
Breathing in my breath grows deep.
Breathing out my breath grows slow.
Deep; slow. (five breaths)
Breathing in I feel calm.
Breathing out I feel relaxed.
Calm; relaxed. (five breaths)
Breathing in I'm aware of the present moment.
Breathing out I know it's a perfect moment.
Present moment; perfect moment.

At the end of the meditation you will notice that your respiration slows, your blood pressure falls, and your heartbeat returns to a normal pace. That's the body. But the changes in mind and spirit are more striking. You become calm and find a quiet place where all is well, peacefully dwelling in the present moment.

One of my clients, Carol, is forty-two years old and facing her third recurrence of cancer. Over a period of nine years it has attacked her brain, her left breast, and now her lungs. This vibrant, energetic mother designs and builds patio furniture, counsels parents with difficult children, teaches a coping skills class for parents who have children with Disassociative Identity Disorder, and is raising two young sons.

When the cancer struck again, she was overcome by fear, anger, and insomnia. We worked together using breath meditations. Her sleeping had improved and her bouts of anger and fear became manageable.

Carol is also claustrophobic. When she has an appointment for an MRI, the anxiety begins several days before the test. She needs a friend in the room with her, and the technician usually pulls her out of the machine three or four times because the fear makes Carol hyperventilate.

I visited Carol the day before her next scheduled MRI and suggested that she imagine herself floating in a calm, cool lake (Carol loves to swim) and do the breath meditation. The next day she went to the hospital alone and was able to stay in the machine for the full fifty-minute test. The technician remarked that Carol was calmer coming out of the machine than before she entered it.

All Carol did was pay attention to her breath, and the present moment became not only bearable but pleasant. Present moment, perfect moment.

Exercise

First, take a couple of really deep breaths, noticing where in the body you feel the breath most clearly. For some it is the air gently caressing the nostrils as it is drawn in and let out; some feel the chest rising and falling; others are aware of the abdomen rising and falling. It doesn't matter where you feel the breath as long as you connect it with the body.

We'll be watching our breath, so don't try to control it by making it deeper or slower. As you pay attention to the breath its characteristics may change—it may get deeper or shallower; it may slow down or quicken; you may notice it more strongly in the abdomen instead of the chest or feel the air entering your nostrils. Just notice the change. Then do the Guided Meditation on page 18. At the silent part, it may be helpful to mentally repeat the key words each time you breathe. For example: inhale—IN, exhale—OUT; inhale—DEEP, exhale—SLOW; inhale—CALM, exhale—RELAXED.

Now that you've located your breath we can work with it further, first as a concentration practice to develop *samadhi* (a deep feeling of calm) by focusing on something, in this case the breath, and ignoring all distractions.

■

SHARPENING THE FOCUS

Counting the Breath

One way to keep our attention on the breath is to count it.

Start by counting each inhalation and exhalation: inhale—ONE, exhale—TWO, and so on, up to ten. Then begin with number one again. The important thing is to watch the breath—the numbers are simply a reference point. As you silently say the numbers, draw the pronunciation out to match the length of an inhalation and exhalation. If your breath is short, the numbers are short; if long, the numbers can be drawn-out—wooooooooon, twoooooooo, threeeeeee.

When your mind wanders or you're distracted by sound, silently note "thinking" and begin counting the breath again, starting with number one. Don't worry that your mind is always busy or that you lose track of the numbers. When you realize that you're thinking or dreaming or planning or worrying, just note "thinking" and begin again.

The mind's job is to think. It doesn't want to be still. It's like a frisky new puppy, poking its nose into everything, doing its business everywhere but on the paper set down on the kitchen floor. We are paper-training our mind to think only when we want it to. Be gentle with yourself—rubbing your nose in your failure won't work. Gently note "thinking" and come back to counting the breath. The mere fact that you notice when you're distracted is training the mind.

When you feel that you can pay attention for five minutes or so, you can make the practice more challenging by counting only the exhalations. Some people think that counting the breath is a simple practice, but it's like building up a bank balance. When difficult times occur, sometimes we're so frazzled that we need the structure of counting or on a simpler level, noting in—out with each breath.

Remember the old saw, when you're angry stop and count to ten? What we're doing is slowing ourselves down, calming ourselves before we act. If we coordinate the numbers with the exhalations, we'll slow down even further. Think of the way football players psych themselves up before a big game by roaring and banging heads and punching lockers. Before an important interview or a meeting with a dying person, I psych myself *down* by counting my breaths. Experiment with this centering breath whenever you are anxious, nervous, angry, or discombobulated.

Mantra

In many spiritual traditions a syllable, word, or phrase is repeated over and over again to help focus the mind, develop concentration, and reach a still point. In the Hindu tradition this is known as a mantra. A well-known Hindu mantra is Om. In the Zen tradition students are often asked to discover the meaning of Mu by repeating the syllable Mu.

Repeating a mantra can be a challenge, because after a time the syllable becomes automatic and we tend to drift off. One way to overcome this robotic repetition is to match the exhalation with Mu or Om. Become the breath, become Om or Mu. At this point our small self falls away and there is just Om, just Mu.

It is possible to create your own phrase or to use a phrase from a prayer. Some Christians use the phrase "Christ have mercy."

Rose is in the hospital because her cancer has metastasized to her hips, and her greatest worry is that she won't be able to take care of her personal needs when she goes home. She pulls a rosary made of rough cord and wooden beads from her pocket and asks me to help her.

Rose is an emigrant from China, and although her English is excellent, she has trouble with the prayers. Could I write the words of the Hail Mary for her? I'm flummoxed—I can barely remember the words. The only way I can grasp them is to mentally rattle them off very quickly and trust that they're imbedded in my memory along with other things learned by rote in childhood, like the multiplication tables or "Incident in a French Camp," by Robert Browning. It works and I repeat the words for Rose.

Because of her distress Rose still can't recall the entire prayer, so we create a mantra for her. As she fingers each bead, she will silently repeat "Hail Mary, full of grace" as she exhales. After several minutes Rose is calmer and feels that Mary will watch over her.

Rose felt a spiritual connection with the Blessed Virgin as she prayed with her rosary. But perhaps it wasn't the words that forged this union with Mary, but the careful attention Rose brought to touching the wooden beads, watching her breath, and aspirating the phrase. The same sense of spiritual connection can be experienced by saying Om or Mu or by counting. The fully focused attention on the breath leads to the calm state of mind that opens us to "allow God's breath to be your breath; allow God's nature to be your nature."

Fingering beads, such as rosary beads or *malas* (the Buddhist equivalent of rosary beads), brings an extra dimension to the meditation—breath, speech, and touch. Although many religions use different kinds of rosaries to count mantras or prayers, to my mind it is touch that helps deepen meditation.

On the sunporch of an adult day-care center, five women in varying stages of Alzheimer's are sitting around a table. In front of each one there are small boxes containing red, yellow, blue, and green wooden beads. Each woman has a heavy extra-long shoelace.

I have already been to each one and helped her locate her breath. We are going to say the names of the colors out loud, drawing the sound out, and then pick up the appropriate bead to string it. Quite loudly, I aspirate Reeeeed and one woman joins me and picks up a red bead and strings it. Yelloooooow. This time another woman joins in—she just likes making the sounds. After the fourth time, everyone is making the sound, four of the five are stringing beads, and two have even strung them in proper sequence.

This is no small thing—for a brief time, five confused women have been in the present moment, connecting to their breath and to each other through hearing, speech, and touch. At later sessions three people are able to follow a more elaborate sequence of colors: red, blue, blue, yellow, green.

Body, speech, and mind all working together for a few clear moments.

Chanting

It's no accident that most spiritual traditions include vocalization in their ceremonies. Whether it's Zen chanting of a scripture, the singing and dancing of Native Americans at a sun ceremony, pristine Gregorian chants, Tibetan toning, a congregation joined together singing hymns, the joyful noise of gospel singing—the result is the same. The throat, chest, and abdomen open, allowing the breath to enter deeply. Saying the words sharpens our attention; the communal sound connects us to one another in harmony.

Exercise

After following your breath for a couple of minutes, begin to say out loud the sound HO. Take a deep breath, and during the exhalation say HO as loudly and deeply as you can, drawing out the sound (and your breath) as long as you can. Repeat the sound several times, really putting yourself into it. When you feel ready, stop and resume your silent meditation practice.

Notice how your breath is deeper after chanting. Notice how your body has rid itself of tensions and sinks into the cushion or chair like a stone. Notice how the aspirated syllable has tethered you to the present moment.

Melinda's autistic son Arthur sometimes gets so agitated that he screams weird sounds at a high pitch and flails his hands around, sometimes hurting himself. It is unsettling for him and is trying for the other family members.

One morning Melinda brought Arthur, his brother Carl, and a couple of other kids to my meditation room at Peaceful Dwelling. We practiced breathing in and breathing out with a little walking meditation. The children particularly enjoyed sounding the various bells that are used to mark the beginning and end of meditation.

We all talked about what to do when we were feeling gnarly and agreed that stopping to take a couple of deep breaths was a way to feel calmer. I suggested that when Arthur felt like screaming he say the sound AH instead, making it as long and deep as possible. It would be his special sound for calming. He tried Ahhing and liked it. When he forgets to use his magic calming tool, Melinda simply says Ahhh, and Arthur joins in.

Whenever you are agitated, try working with your breath. Release the emotion in a deep sigh or count your breaths or match your breath to a mantra. The breath is always available to calm us.

Going Deeper

I'm trying to count my breaths, but I can't seem to get to number ten; I'm always thinking about something.

It takes quite a while for most of us to tame the mind. Sometimes you will hear Buddhists refer to "Monkey Mind." The metaphor likens the mind to a monkey, always swinging from one tree to another, grabbing at bananas, and jabbering away. Our Monkey Mind grabs at thoughts, sounds, anything that might be entertaining.

Don't be harsh with yourself. It may be helpful to think of your mind as an endearing, but mischievous pet. Give your monkey a name, like Fred. When you notice that thoughts are arising, just note "there's Fred" with a patient smile, and come back to the feeling of your breath going in and out and begin counting again.

There's nothing special about the number ten. Try counting to six instead. When you feel you have the hang of it, then move up to ten. Remember to silently say the number, drawing out the sound to match the length of your inhalation and exhalation. We are watching our breath and labeling it, not counting.

I seem able to count my out-breaths up to ten fairly consistently, but now I'm bored.

Your mind has been paper-trained and is now ready to heel. Try counting just the exhalations up to 100. When your mind wanders, start at number one. If you get to 100, let the numbers go.

Carefully watch the rhythm of your breath by following it very closely. Pay attention to every nuance. Is the inhalation shorter than the exhalation? Is the breath smooth or ragged, fast or slow, deep or shallow, warm or cool? Let yourself be carried by the rhythm of the breath. It's like floating on a gentle wave in the ocean. Follow the rhythm of the breath; follow the rhythm of your life.

I've been working with a mantra and sometimes I feel that I'm in a nice, safe place where everything is pleasant. Is this what meditation is supposed to feel like?

There's no "supposed to" in meditation, or in life. Each time we sit, the experience is different. One of my teachers taught over and over again, "Expect nothing!" Simply pay attention to what is arising.

The safe place that you enjoy may mean that you've reached a deeper level of concentration, but be vigilant. If you get to a place that you think is wonderful, be careful not to get attached to it.

Sometimes this space is really just a distraction that the mind sets up. It's like being in a canoe—you paddle along and then take your oar out of the water and lie back enjoying the pleasant day. But eventually you realize that your canoe has wandered off course, so it's time to put your oar back in. When this happens in meditation, it's time to put more energy into your practice.

As you say your mantra, meticulously prolong the sound to match your exhalation. It may be hard to let go of the dreamy space, but by dipping the oar in the water you will go deeper and discover a place beyond pleasant. Try to become your mantra.

In *Ch'an* meditation (the Chinese form of Zen) there is a practice called *hua-tou*. You are given a conundrum to penetrate. You work on it like a mantra, but when your mind quiets and you become intimate with your *hua-tou*, the answer arises spontaneously. You may want to try working on one of your own questions—Who am I? Where did I come from? Where am I going? What is it?

Many years ago, at the beginning of my Zen studies my teacher gave me a difficult koan (a conundrum like *hua-tou*) to meditate on. It was way beyond my capabilities, but since I would be attending a ten-day retreat, he thought it would be an interesting challenge.

When I spoke to the retreat's teacher, she said, "I don't know what your teacher had in mind—why don't you meditate on this instead, 'What is my life's work?'" I was disappointed because I thought this was the opportunity to impress my own teacher with my understanding and progress. But I did as she suggested. I meditated on "What is my life's work?" the whole time, and each day when I had a brief private meeting with the teacher, I would present an answer, sure that I had gotten it. Each time she'd say "More!" or "Wonderful, go deeper!" until on the final day I presented my last answer, and she said, "Now I believe you!"

As I sat on the deck of the ferry taking me back home, I realized that she had distilled the elaborate koan my teacher had given me into that one phrase. The answer was the same.

Finding the right question to ask can open the door to finding the answer. Follow your breath mindfully for a couple of minutes and see if a question arises.

I usually sit in a chair because I have a bad back, and I try to concentrate on my breath, but before I know it, I'm nodding off.

First, check your sitting position. It's not a good idea to try to sit on a sofa or soft chair. Choose a straight-backed chair. Your back should be erect but relaxed and not leaning against the back of the chair. Place your feet flat on the floor about shoulder-width apart and position your hands in your lap. You may need to place a cushion beneath your feet so that your knees are at the same level as your hips.

If sleepiness still arises, note "sleepiness" and come back to your practice. If you have been sitting with your eyes closed, open them and gaze at the floor at a forty-five-degree angle. Put more energy into your practice. For example, if you are working with the breath, begin to label each inhalation and exhalation as "in," "out." If the group where you are practicing allows it, as a final resort stand up. It's very difficult to sleep while standing!

Try not to judge yourself as a "bad" meditator just because you're sleepy. Each of us has our own body clock—some have difficulty early in the morning, others at night; and post-lunch meditation is sluggish for everyone. It's just another chance to be mindful of what is arising. "Oh, sleepiness is arising, how interesting!"

Begin to notice the feelings that come up about being sleepy—annoyance, judgment, frustration, despair. Be mindful of what is happening right now, in the present moment. Who knows, you just may be tired!

I can't count, I can't sit still, and I really hate doing this!

Congratulations! You've just met three of the five traditional hindrances up close and personal and it's a perfect cue for us to examine them in detail on page 29.

⋄ The best way to learn something is to teach it to others. Choose a person or small group wishing to learn Mindfulness of Breathing (page 18) and guide them.

⋄ If you work with children, the elderly, emotionally disturbed adults, or another group, try inventing additional phrases of your own that might be meaningful or helpful to them. When I worked with schizophrenics, guiding was necessary because when they were silent for long periods, some heard voices in their heads. Generally, the voices sent negative messages, inciting the patients to harm themselves physically. Even with medication, the voices can prevail, arousing fear and anxiety. I would begin with the mindfulness of breathing exercise (page 18) and create additional empowering phrases that would supplant the negative voices.

> Breathing in I am like the sun.
> Breathing out I feel bright.
> Sun; Bright.
> Breathing in I am like a mountain.
> Breathing out I feel strong.
> Mountain; Strong.
> Breathing in I am like the sky.
> Breathing out I am clear.
> Sky; Clear.
> Breathing in I am like the ocean.
> Breathing out I am deep.
> Ocean; Deep.

⋄ Each time the phone rings, use it as a signal to notice one full inhalation and exhalation before picking it up.

⋄ Create your own mantra for difficult situations.

⋄ Use an old necklace or search yard sales for interesting beads and make your own mala. If you are counting your breaths, use ten beads with one larger bead or a tassel. If you are using a mantra, string thirty-three or 108 beads, the traditional numbers.

⋄ If you've decided to work on a koan or *hua-tou*, carry it into your daily life. When you're walking or working out at the gym or gardening, every once in a while come back to the sensation of your breath going in and out and state your question. For example: Step, step, step, step, step, step, "Who am I?"

⋄ Carry a small stone in your pocket. Each time you touch it, stop and take a couple of mindful breaths.

■

THE HINDRANCES

Desire, aversion/anger, doubt, restlessness, along with (my own personal favorite) sloth and torpor are the hindrances that come up when we try to meditate. Everyone has to deal with each of them at one time or another. They are often thought of as barriers that keep us from awakening.

Instead of viewing the hindrances as the enemy, think of them as helping to make our meditation more stable. If they didn't arise, we would have nothing to practice with. First we learn to work with restlessness or aversion in our sitting practice, and when pain, suffering, fear, or imminent death confronts us in our daily life we are ready to face it.

A friend calls the hindrances the Buddha's five dwarfs—Greedy, Grumpy, Antsy, Sleepy, and Doubtful. Hi! Ho! Hi! Ho! It's off to work we go.

Desire

The Buddha taught that desire is the cause of all suffering. We want what we want when we want it, and when we don't get it, we suffer. If we do get what we want, we grow attached to it and worry that we'll lose it—suffering. If we get something we don't want, then we get angry—suffering. So when a tiny desire arises during meditation, it's helpful to note it before we get carried away.

You may be sitting with a few friends, trying to follow your breath and a gentle breeze wafts in through an open window. You notice the sensation of the cool breeze on your face while simultaneously feeling the sun's warmth. "Isn't it pleasant! I'd rather be outside," desire pipes up. Your meditation has been very calming, but now you want something better. Then a cloud covers the sun and you become chilly. "I wish I had my sweater."

Most of us live our lives like Goldilocks, judging our porridge as too hot or too cold. When we find a bowl that's just right, we eat it all up wanting more, and desire escalates into greed. Our lives are filled with chasing after more, most, and better, best. We are forever trying to change our circumstances, thinking that will make us happy. But the secret of happiness is appreciating what we have.

Lucy was a Puerto Rican nurse who had worked in a cancer hospital until she herself developed breast cancer. She was admitted to the hospital many times, always returning to my floor. Although Lucy was Pentecostal Christian, she welcomed my visits, and over several months I watched her deteriorate.

Lucy was a whiner—the food was no good, the nurses harsh; she questioned the doctors' protocols. It was her way of coping, and I thought that probably when my turn came to experience sickness, old age, and death that would be my way, too.

As the cancer spread to her bones and spine, Lucy needed surgery. For over a week she was fed intravenously and could not move. I visited her when her first solid meal was being served.

A tangerine glittered like a jewel on a tray cluttered with gray mystery meat, rice, overcooked vegetables, Wonder bread, and pudding. Lucy's eyes lit up when she noticed the tangerine and, because her hands trembled, she asked me to peel it for her. As my nails broke the skin, its wonderful fragrance burst forth and the room exuded tangerineness. Lucy drank in the aroma and said, "Aaaah!"

As if it were the first time she had ever seen or smelled a tangerine, she experienced it fully. In the midst of her pain, she was able to be grateful for what she had and appreciate what was wonderful in life.

Sometimes during a retreat we fall in love with a person sitting across the room. We don't know his or her name or anything about them. We just fall in love. Desire becomes lust. But it's just a thought.

You can weave a fantasy about the mysterious object of desire or you can burrow under the story and face the neediness, longing, and emptiness that clamor for attention. Usually we pacify the deep feeling of being disconnected by feeding it food, drugs, fantasies. Or we distract ourselves by making busywork or turning on the TV or surfing the Net. But these strategies don't work for very long.

When we sit still, quietly following our breath, desire surfaces with a vengeance—I need something to make me feel good; I need something to make me feel complete; I need something, anything to fill the deep hole in my heart.

The next time you notice "wanting" during meditation, drop the story. It doesn't matter what you want. The feeling of desire is the same whether it's for a more comfortable chair or a new car or someone to love us. It's just a matter of degree.

All we have to do is note "wanting" or "desire" and focus on the sensation that arises in our body. Then we'll realize that the wanting is just a thought—we don't have to obey it. Working with tiny urges trains us so that when really deep lust for a person, place, or thing emerges from the depths of our neediness, we'll be able to look it in the face and note, "It's just a thought."

Aversion/Anger

I would be able to count my breaths up to 100 if only the person sitting next to me wasn't breathing so hard. Maybe I can leave an anonymous note under his cushion telling him that he's ruining the meditation for everybody else. I wonder if there are any empty seats—maybe I can move after the lunch break. What's wrong with him? Why doesn't the teacher say something? If he doesn't shut up, I'll kill him.

This is aversion. We are irked by a fly buzzing around our head and try to wave it away. When that doesn't work, we swat at the fly, killing it. If we don't take care of a niggling annoyance, it can escalate into full-fledged rage and result in harm to ourselves and others. Many divorces start this way; most wars start this way. What would happen if we simply noted "aversion" or "anger" when a thought like that came up and we sat paying rapt attention to the place in the body where the anger seemed to lodge?

Working with the insignificant irritations that arise during meditation is one thing, but when we quiet down and reach a still place, old angers, resentments, and hurts can crop up. We work with anger at our boss or resentment at being abused or rage at life's unfairness in the same way we deal with the petty irritations that occur during sitting—by paying attention to the sensations in our bodies.

On the first day of a week-long retreat, as I was sitting quietly, feeling centered and calm, I noticed a sharp pain. It felt like the talons of a bird of prey gripping my left shoulder. Sometimes it became strong so I needed to place my full attention there, noticing if it was concentrated or diffuse, hot or cold, sharp or dull. Other times the pain hovered in the background. I carried it for a couple of days, feeling like Long John Silver. I knew it was a psychic pain, because I had not injured my shoulder in any way.

One afternoon as I was doing walking meditation, I looked down at my feet and was filled with gratitude for being able to walk and breathe and be alive. Tears of joy flowed down my face.

When I sat down during the next meditation period, I realized the pain in my shoulder was gone, and with it a deep resentment that I had been carrying around for over a year. I wanted to let it go, I knew my life would be better if I let it go, I knew that I should let it go. Still it held on. During the retreat, by staying with the sensation of tightness in my shoulder, not dredging up the story of why I felt resentment, *it* let go of me. It was such a relief, feeling the talons loosening and the raptor flying off. Freedom.

Once you get past the natural hesitancy to deal with anger (aversion to aversion), it becomes easier to stay with our major hurts. Then you can realize that one can't be angry and joyful at the same time.

Rage and anger are the major cohorts of aversion, but what about the supporting cast: resentment, hurt, frustration, irritation, annoyance, impatience, and boredom?

Over the years I've gotten better at dealing with big stuff, but I'm still impatient—things never happen when I think they should, people don't act in the way I think they should, life isn't what I think it should be. It seems that if we can remove the word *should* from our vocabulary, we can take care of a lot of aversion as well.

At first boredom doesn't look like aversion or anger, but when we probe further we can see that when things aren't exciting or challenging enough, we become angry that things are not the way we wish them to be—aversion masquerades as boredom.

When we succumb to aversion, we give up our own power and subject ourselves to the vicissitudes of life. We become victims of people and circumstances. Looking at the feelings that arise when things don't go our way helps us to take responsibility for our lives and give up the expectation that others can make our lives perfect.

Restlessness

Many new meditators say they just can't sit still. Sometimes the need to move is caused by physical discomfort—your legs have fallen asleep or your back hurts. The temptation to move just a tiny bit is overwhelming. The seeds are desire—wanting to be comfortable, and aversion—pushing away discomfort.

Can you stay with the desire to move for just a little while? Can you look at it the same way you look at a thought, noting "sensation"? Can you arouse curiosity about the sensation—is it hot or cool, prickling or stabbing or throbbing, widespread or concentrated?

When the full attention is engaged, the pain becomes just sensation and you are able to stay with it without moving. If we are not able to be with small discomfort, how will we react if we break a leg or have a heart attack or develop cancer?

Here is an ancient Zen story:

Some monks were standing in the courtyard of their monastery, looking at the banner flying from the rampart. A monk asked the teacher, "Is it the flag moving, or is it the wind?"

The teacher answered, "It is your mind that is moving."

It is our mind that names sensation as pleasant or unpleasant, that turns pain into suffering. Practice staying with discomfort and you'll be training the mind to stay with what is happening in the present moment, without attachment or aversion.

Sometimes the body just won't stay still. Your foot wants to move, your nose wants to twitch, your hands need to scratch an imaginary itch. You're filled with nervous energy and you can't concentrate on your practice. The urge to move may be over-powering, even though nothing itches or tickles or hurts. Ask yourself, "What am I moving away from?"

While attending a retreat I kept noticing that I was moving my fingers, readjusting my posture and shrinking back. Nothing hurt. Why couldn't I be still? I sunk into the sensation, the feeling of wanting to pull back, to tuck myself into a ball and disappear. After a while I began to experience fear and I knew that my mind did not want to deal with it. The fear grew and consumed me until

I began to shake and cry. I sat with the terror for a couple of days. Psychotherapists tell us that under anger lies sadness and lurking below is fear. Coming face to face with nameless terror was not fun or easy, but when it slunk away, I felt gratitude and freedom.

The mind gets restless too. The Monkey Mind refuses to be tamed. It hops around trying to do its job, which is to think. Remember who's boss. Just note "restlessness" and return to your practice of following the breath.

We obsessively plan the future or worry about it, rather than staying in the present moment, being aware of the breath going in and out, the chest rising and falling. NOW is all we have and restlessness carries us away into the future. When restlessness arises, notice it and return to the present moment.

Doubt

Two kinds of doubt arise when we meditate. The first, great doubt—Who am I? What is the meaning of life? Why am I here?—focuses our attention and helps us go deeper. Other doubts seek to erode our confidence: I'll never be able to do this right. Maybe I should try a different kind of meditation or teacher or group. Why am I doing this?

When these thoughts creep into our meditation, treat them the same way you treat all the hindrances. Note "doubting" and return to the sensation of your breath going in and out.

Janet leads a busy life. She has a ten-year-old son and an adopted Vietnamese baby girl. She runs a thriving gardening business sandwiched between driving her son to and from school and assorted clubs and sports activities. The baby goes back and forth to the sitter. Twice a week she picks vegetables at an organic farm. In addition to food shopping, cleaning the house, and preparing most meals, she teaches Sunday school.

Janet meets with a small group once a week to meditate. This special time helps her to calm her anxieties and remain centered in the midst of her schedule. Yet during the spring, her busiest season, doubt creeps into her meditation: I should be ordering plants. Maybe I should be taking the baby for a stroll. I forgot to buy bread for supper.

Each of these nudging thoughts undermines her desire to meditate. Instead of buckling under, she faces the doubts and continues to meet with her meditation group, secure in the knowledge that this time is necessary to balance her life.

Doubt is wishy-washy. It has no conviction or courage. That has to come from you. The more you practice, the more courage you'll find to face doubt not only as a hindrance to meditation, but as a hindrance in your life. Choices become more clear-cut. The path we take in our daily life opens up and decisions are easier.

Sloth and Torpor

This hindrance frequently manifests itself as sleepiness. Outright sleepiness can be dealt with—sitting erect, opening your eyes, putting more emphasis on counting the breath, standing up, or splashing cold water on your face. Sloth and torpor are subtle culprits. We allow ourselves to become dreamy as if we're floating on a still lake, trailing our fingers in the water. It may feel comfortable, even pleasant, but it's not meditation.

Meditation is not trance or spacing out; it is a vibrant, living practice. The goal is to be awake; to be mindful of everything life offers—the pleasant and unpleasant. Paying full attention to whatever arises.

Have you ever seen a deer in the forest? It stands as still as a statue until a twig crackles. Then it comes alive. This is the kind of alertness we can bring to our meditation. Sloth makes us lazy and torpor makes us complacent. It takes effort to bring our attention back to our practice each time our mind wanders.

A student asked a sage, "What is practice?"
The sage answered, "Attention!"

"I know that. What else is there?" the student asked.

The sage repeated, "Attention!"

The student persisted, "There must be more!"

The sage roared, "Attention! Attention! Attention!"

Twenty years ago, I planted ivy in a brick container attached to my house. The ivy grew lush and thick, covering the brick base of the house, and began to trail up the cedar shingles. It looked wonderful.

But last spring when I was moving a shrub, I noticed that tendrils had insinuated themselves under and between the shingles. The luxuriant growth was strangling my house. I had to rip it off and it resisted. It took a lot of energy to strip off two truckloads of vines.

At first the house looked naked, but gradually I got used to its being pristine and bare. But in the late summer as I was deadheading the lilies, I noticed the vines beginning to snake up the shingles once again.

The hindrances are like that ivy. When we pay careful attention to desire, anger, restlessness, doubt, sluggishness, or whatever may arise, we notice it and can take care of it at that moment. We don't have to wait until we're engulfed by it, like my house hidden by the ivy.

I've dealt with all of the hindrances at one time or another in my own meditation practice. It's a never-ending task—there's always a new shoot ready to twine itself around true nature and suffocate it. But now I've learned to pull away the tendrils lovingly—they are friends who let me know where I am in my practice. When one of them shows up unexpectedly, I remember the lyrics of a Billie Holiday song. "Good morning heartache, my old friend—sit down."

Making the Practice Your Own

⬧ The next time you want something simple, say another cup of tea, take a few moments to notice where the desire resides. Pay attention to the sensations in your body while following your breath. Do you still want the tea?

◆ Choose an object that you think you can't possibly part with. Put it in a closet or the garage or attic or basement for one week. Did you miss it? After a couple of days, did you notice it wasn't there?

◆ If you become furious at someone, before you act make a list of all the bad qualities the person has. Then make a check mark next to each negative trait that you also share. Next, write down her good qualities. Make a check mark next to those you have. Can you find some common ground?

■

WIDENING THE FOCUS

After some time counting the breath, we develop a solid base of concentration and then we can broaden the focus. Whatever is our predominant experience in the present moment becomes the object of meditation. The sounds of a dog barking or a radio playing or a truck rumbling by are no longer distractions—they are the focus of our meditation.

Guided Meditation

Take a couple of deep breaths, being aware of your breath going in and out, feeling your chest rising and falling.

For a few moments keep your attention on the breath, then gradually allow the ambient sounds to come into your awareness. Notice the songs of birds, the wind blowing, the clink of a radiator, the noise of traffic.

Open to each sound as it enters your awareness, without naming the source. Simply feel the sound in your body. Pay careful attention as a sound comes nearer, as it reaches its peak, and as it fades away. Let the sound become a part of you.

Return to your breath when the sound disappears, leaving yourself open and willing to receive the next sound. If you become enthralled by a sound, occasionally note "hearing" to keep your attention sharp.

If there are several sounds, just stay with whatever is predominant.

Try to expand the field of attention by opening to body sensations as well. There are always sensations in the body; we just don't pay attention to them.

Do a body scan from head to toe. As you bring your attention to your head, what do you notice? Is it heavy or light? Do you notice vibration or tingling or stiffness? Follow your breath for a few moments, letting the sensation in your head become apparent. When you are ready, move down your neck, shoulders, arms, hands, and fingers, then down your back, chest, and stomach, continuing down your hips, legs, feet, and toes, noting the sensation in each body part.

Then return to the breath before opening your eyes.

When you placed your attention on sounds, did you notice that they became interesting, not just distractions? As you moved your awareness throughout your body, did you discover sensations you had not realized were there?

When we are ready to widen the focus of meditation, everything in our life becomes interesting and a source of wonder. We begin to wake up to the vibrancy of everything in us and around us. Sounds are us; sensations are us. We are everything; everything is us.

We can go further. Without identifying a sound (bird, truck), note "hearing." When any physical sensation becomes apparent, note "sensation." When a thought arises, note "thinking." When a smell drifts into consciousness, note "smelling."

We are practicing taking in everything, rejecting nothing.

This is the basis of using meditation for pain management. After practicing this way of experiencing pain, we may want to call it "pain appreciation" or "sensation awareness."

Exercise—Working with Physical Pain

Begin to meditate by watching your breath going in and out for a period of time.

Then bring your attention to your feet touching the floor, and notice how they are rooted to the earth.

Now bring your attention to your hands. Notice the weight of your hands. Notice them touching your lap. Are they warm or cool?

Notice that when you place your attention on your hands you can really feel them. You may become aware of tingling or warmth.

Stay with the sensation for a time.

Is there any part of your body that is tense or painful?

If so, bring your awareness to the uncomfortable area.

Place your full attention on the sensation.

Is it concentrated or diffused?

Is it tingling or sharp or throbbing or stabbing or numb or tight?

Is the area large or small?

As you focus your complete attention on the sensation, does it change?

Does it become stronger or weaker?

Larger or smaller?

Keep focusing on the sensation. When your mind wanders, return to the feeling of your breath going in and out.

Most people who try this notice that the sensation changes when they pay attention to it. It may get stronger, but then it weakens. The sensation ebbs and flows. It is not a solid, permanent object. It will not always be with us. Everything changes, even pain.

The same technique of mindful awareness can be used to work with emotional pain as well.

How does anger feel or sadness or loss?

For many years anger, with all its themes and variations, has been my biggest hindrance. I feel my neck stiffen and my jaw tighten. Other people feel a knot in their gut, or their blood pressure rises and their face feels hot and flushed. Sometimes the aversion is so overwhelming that all we can do is cry tears of frustration. Once, I began to feel my sinuses fill up, my nostrils tighten as the pinpricks of tears arose. Then my eyes puddled with moisture and became hot and irritated. I noticed my desire not to cry, not wanting anyone to see my emotions. But then one tear leaked out of the corner of my eye. It started out feeling hot, but as it slowly slid down my cheeks, the air cooled it and the single drop became cold. When it finally dripped off my chin onto my shirt the anger was gone too. But the trace of the tear remained—a cool, sticky snail's path down my right cheek.

Try to "just sit," noticing whatever is predominant in your experience. A sound enters consciousness—stay with it until something more pressing occurs, for example, a sensation in your leg. Then a thought arises. Note "thinking" without getting involved in the story. A hindrance arrives, sleepiness. Go to the sensation of sleepiness in the body, noting "sleepy." Another thought appears and your mind is off and running, chasing a fantasy. As soon as you notice, silently say "thinking" and come back to the feeling of your breath going in and out.

During this "just sitting" meditation, the breath is in the background, acting as an anchor whenever we drift off course. Follow your breath for a time, then open your awareness to include sound and sensations. It's like using a microscope. We're constantly making adjustments so that our vision is clear.

We can fine-tune our awareness further by noticing the quality of our thoughts, emotions, and sensations by labeling them as pleasant, unpleasant, or neutral. This keeps us from getting entangled in attachment or aversion and lessens the likelihood of judging ourselves and our experiences.

Whether you sharpen your focus by concentrating on the breath or widen it to include sounds, sensations, or emotions, you are practicing mindfulness. In the next chapter we will learn to bring that awareness to our daily lives.

Making the Practice Your Own

◈ At your next meal, pay attention to the feel and weight of your fork as you pick it up. Notice how your food looks on the plate. Then, as you taste the first bite, note "tasting." Is the food hot, tepid, or cool? Is it spicy or bland or sweet or salty? Is the texture chewy, soft, tough, or crunchy?

◈ Cradle a cup of tea in both hands, noticing the warmth of the cup in your hands, inhaling the aroma, watching the steam curl out of the cup, appreciating the color of the tea. Then taste it. Appreciate it. AAAH!

◈ Try the body scan. This time, as each sensation becomes known, label it pleasant, unpleasant, or neutral.

Four

Moving Meditation

MINDFULNESS IN EVERYDAY LIFE

It is a cloudy summer day and there are sixteen of us walking in a line on a trail beside a narrow stream. We are just across the street from the adult day-care center where we usually meditate indoors, but this nature trail has carried us into a different world.

The emotionally disadvantaged adults in this group range in age from twenty-one to sixty. Some are schizophrenic, some manic-depressive, some slightly retarded, some asocial. Most have abused or are still abusing drugs and alcohol. All have that sleepy, puffy, heavy appearance that identifies people taking antipsychotics and serves to isolate them further from "normal" people.

The staff at the center has warned me that some people in the group come to meditation because they can cop a nap. Perhaps that was true at the beginning, but I don't believe it's true now.

We are walking at a slow pace, placing each foot carefully, mindful that the earth is a part of us. Each silently says the word *touching* as a foot touches the earth. When someone notices an interesting object—a flower or rock or, once, ants crawling over discarded food, he calls, "Look!" and we all gather around, experiencing the object with our full attention while following our breath. After a minute or two, I say, "Let's walk," and we continue along the trail.

Thirty minutes later we are back in the anonymous meeting room and talk about the walking meditation. "I never noticed that tree had roots in the water before." "The ground was squishy." "That's moss, it's supposed to be like that." "It was like dancing." "Let's go tomorrow, too." "I really liked that tree's roots."

For a brief time some of the group, having noticed their surroundings, connected with nature and became a part of the world.

WALKING

In many Eastern spiritual traditions, walking is considered as important as sitting. At most of the retreats that Peaceful Dwelling offers, we practice individual mindful walking, preferably outside. But sometimes the weather doesn't cooperate or there is no suitable outdoor space. Walking meditation can certainly be practiced indoors.

At a loving-kindness retreat held for cancer survivors at a support center in Manhattan, we practiced walking meditation indoors. We walked slowly in a circle and were told to say one of the metta keywords (see Chapter Four) with each step. After a time people fell into a natural rhythm of following in the footsteps of the person in front of them. We became one entity, just stepping, stepping, our legs and feet moving as one, like a centipede. It illustrated beautifully one teacher's encouraging instruction, "We are practicing alone, together."

By alternating sitting and walking meditation periods of equal duration, there is less stress on the body. Usually there are two weak points in sitting meditation that can cause physical discomfort or pain (or as we learned to call it in the last chapter, "sensation")—the knees and the back. When people are already dealing with pain from chemotherapy or their medical symptoms, meditation won't work if it brings additional suffering. Walking meditation, especially outdoors, is a welcome respite for those who are ill and lifts their spirits.

There are several good reasons for doing walking meditation:

◇ After sitting for some time, legs fall asleep, knees ache, and backs tighten. Walking gives our bodies time to recuperate (and to use the restroom).

◇ Walking balances our energy—if we are sleepy, it wakes us up; if we are restless, it calms us down, bringing us back to our center.

◇ Walking is a bridge between sitting meditation and our daily lives. It helps us to know that we can carry the focus and quiet attention acquired during sitting into our daily activities.

◇ The most compelling reason to practice walking meditation is the walking itself. We connect with our bodies in a more intimate way, paying attention to the expansion and contraction of each muscle, feeling the energy flow through our bodies, sensing the rhythm of life.

Many people protest that they have tried to meditate but cannot concentrate or sit still. Coordinating physical movement with breathing and a mantra offers an opportunity to experience the meditative state for those who have not been able to concentrate while sitting. Perhaps sitting meditation has been difficult for you. I would encourage you to stick with it, but you might also try walking meditation.

Exercise

Directly after sitting meditation, stay seated for a moment. Then form the intention to stand up mindfully. As you rise from your cushion or chair, notice your body shifting as the burden of your weight moves into your legs and feet.

Stand quietly for a moment or two, placing your feet about shoulder-width apart. Slowly shift all your weight to your right foot. Now move your weight back to center. Shift the weight to your left foot, noticing in detail how the weight seems to move down your leg into your foot, as if you're pouring sand into a vase. Then shift back to center.

Notice how delightful it feels. Whenever we take a step, this shifting of weight occurs. Each time we take a step, the muscles of our feet and legs contract and expand. Our body parts the air, just as it slices through the water in swimming. We are just too busy to appreciate it.

Exercise

Choose a space about twenty feet long for your walking. This will be your path. In this meditation the object of attention will be the movement of your feet and legs, rather than the breath. Hold your hands in a position that's comfortable for you—hanging loosely at your sides, clasped in front of your waist or behind your back, or in your pockets. It may be helpful to take shorter strides than you normally would. Keep your eyes open.

Walk back and forth a few times at a normal pace, noticing each time a foot touches the floor. You may want to silently say "touching" or "stepping."

After some time, begin to slow your pace, noticing how your weight shifts from side to side as you step. If your hands are by your sides, you may become aware that they are moving, too. Notice how pleasant it feels to be moving naturally, without trying to get anywhere.

After a little while, slow your pace still further and place the attention on each movement needed to take a step.

Be aware of lifting the heel, moving the foot forward, and placing the foot on the floor. Carefully pay attention to each step.

You may want to silently note "lifting," "moving," "placing" with each motion.

If your mind wanders, stop; take a couple of deep breaths, feeling your breath going in and out; and then continue walking.

After the constraint of sitting still for twenty or thirty minutes, walking feels good. It's important to carry the mindfulness of breathing, sensations, emotions, and thoughts into the walking. What makes walking meditation unique is that we're not trying to get somewhere; we're content to stay in the present moment, carefully watching every movement we make. There is no final destination—it's the process that's important. We are already there.

Going Deeper

When I move very slowly, I tend to lose my balance.

This is a common occurrence when we move slowly. When it happens, stop for a moment and center yourself. Then walk at a medium pace for a while. It may also help to keep your feet shoulder-width apart and make very short strides.

What should I do when I come to the end of my path and need to turn around?

You can simply note "turning" or refine your attention further. Notice how your weight shifts to one foot when you prepare to turn and how, as you take each turning step, the weight shifts back and forth. After completing the turn, you may want to take a couple of breaths before you begin walking again.

After some time I realize that I'm not saying "lifting, moving, placing," but I feel totally aware of each movement. It feels good. Is this okay?

The words are simply a tool to help you concentrate more easily. When you are focused, they will naturally drop away. However, it is easy to fall into a trance-like state—the hypnotic rhythm of slow walking can do this. Make sure that your attention is sharp. When you reach the end of your path, stop and change your focus to standing still for a moment or two. Then continue walking.

I find moving like this maddening and I want to stop.

The hindrances arise in walking, too. It's natural to experience desire, aversion, doubt, restlessness, and even torpor when walking. You work with them the same way you work with the hindrances in sitting meditation. Stop walking (this is easy, you probably want do this anyway) and pay attention to the place in your body where you experience resistance. As it subsides, continue walking.

When we are sitting in a group meditating, we rarely get up if we're uncomfortable or don't feel like meditating anymore—the group energy sustains us and we stay until the bell has sounded. Walking meditation can be more challenging at first because we are on our own—there's no one to chide us if we stop to rest or have a glass of water.

Be gentle with yourself. If it's the first time you've done this type of walking, don't plan to walk for forty minutes. Walk for ten minutes, then stop and sit for a while or have a cup of tea. Then return to your walking. Choose a specific amount of time you'll walk—five minutes or ten or fifteen and stick to it for the whole period.

I try and try, but I can't walk so slowly!

During my first long retreat that consisted of 50 percent sitting and 50 percent walking, I thought I would go mad. I talk fast, think fast, and walk fast. When it was time to walk, I dreaded it. No matter how much I slowed myself down, I was still moving quickly. On my fourth trip along my "path" I'd notice that the person beside me was still on his first trip!

I had to deal with the judging mind that told me I wasn't doing as well as the guy next to me. I had forgotten that this is not a competition. Each of us has an inner tachometer and that is what we work with. After a couple of years my pace slowed, but there was always someone moving more slowly, with itsy-bitsy steps. I had to drop comparing.

Pay careful attention to your steps at the pace you *are* going. You'll naturally slow down when you're ready, not before. We are not trying to change anything, we are just noticing how things are at this moment.

I hate doing walking meditation! Why can't I just do sitting meditation?
During the many retreats and workshops that I've given for professional caregivers, I've found that the majority of attendees have resistance to this kind of walking. Many of them are Type A personalities, used to a speedy way of life. If they reach a place of calm in sitting meditation, they do not want to lose it. So here we have an example of suffering—attachment leads to aversion and then to fear of losing what we have.

We need to trust the process. We need to trust ourselves. If we can achieve serenity in sitting, we can achieve it in walking as well. What good is the measure of calm we attain while sitting on a cushion if we can't carry it into our daily lives? Walking can help us make the transition from the meditation hall to the workplace or home.

Frequently, someone who seems incapable of doing sitting meditation is able to meditate while walking. My old friend Matt, a respected psychotherapist, knows it would be good to meditate and when he does, he feels great. He has attended workshops and retreats, read books, listened to tapes, and even bought a special set of meditation cushions, but is still unable to incorporate meditation into his daily schedule.

At a one-day retreat he was introduced to walking meditation. During retreats, I notice that sometimes people interpret walking periods to mean break time. I see people wandering through the building, sitting quietly drinking coffee, or strolling the gardens. But Matt practiced assiduously—"lifting, moving, placing." At the end of the day during the closing circle, he exclaimed in awe, "I've been walking all my life and never realized that I was walking *on* something. I never felt the ground before."

Matt felt connected to the earth and his body and was able to develop a daily walking practice.

Perhaps you'll discover that walking works for you. Some people experience a true oneness with the world around them while walking, because the body, mind, and spirit are totally engaged in paying attention.

I visited a Zen center and we walked in line very quickly. The pace was too fast for me to note "lifting, moving, placing" and I lost my concentration.

At Zen centers, sitting meditation periods can be thirty, forty, or sixty minutes long, interspersed with a ten-minute walking meditation period called *kinhin*. Unlike the individual mindful walking we practiced before, people walk in a line, following a leader who carries wooden clappers. A common sequence could be CLAP (everyone bows and turns right), CLAP (begin walking very slowly), after a minute or two CLAP (walking speeds up considerably), and so on.

Although it may seem robotic at first, the structure of *kinhin* helps us focus the attention on walking. We don't have to think about where to place our hands. There is only one position, called *sasshu* (left hand forms a loose fist with the thumb curled inside, while the right hand lightly covers it; the clasped hands are held about waist high). We don't have to think about how slowly or quickly to walk. We don't have to decide whether to stop or rest or take a nap. We just walk.

For most people it is easier to concentrate while walking slowly—we reach a comfortable space when we begin to enjoy the rhythmic motion of the legs and feet. Sometimes this may feel like meditation, but we're really drifting, one of the variations of the hindrance sloth/torpor. So, kinhin uses the skillful means of walking more quickly to raise our energy level and keep us alert.

One way to keep your attention focused on the fast walking is to count your steps, one through ten, just as you count your breaths. When your mind wanders, go back to number one. Another way is to simply note "stepping" with each step. When all else fails, you can silently say to yourself "left, right" as if you were marching.

One of the best things about the fast walking of kinhin is that when it's time to sit on your cushion or chair, you welcome it! How quickly aversion turns to desire.

I've been using a mantra during my meditation. How can I work with it during walking?
Mantra and walking meditation work well together to develop concentration. With each step, say your one- or two-syllable mantra instead of "stepping." If it is a long phrase, say it only every other step or shorten the phrase. It is possible to practice your mantra while doing almost any rhythmic sport.

Many years ago, for a now unfathomable reason, I decided to do a triathlon—one-and-a-half-mile deep water swim, twenty-five-mile bike, ten-mile run. I took three months off from work in order to train. I could not swim, and I hadn't ridden a bike for twenty years. All I could do was run long distances, albeit slowly.

A swimming instructor taught me to breathe every third stroke, and I easily fell into a meditative rhythm while completing laps in a pool. At the time I worked with "Mu," and each time I exhaled in the water, I exhaled Mu. On the third stroke, my head turned out of the water to take in air. It felt as if I were taking in all of life, taking in Mu, allowing Mu to sustain me, to be a part of me. And with the next two strokes I let it go. Being born with each in-breath, dying with each out-breath. Becoming totally new with each breath.

Since then, when I periodically join a fitness center, I practice Mu while exercising. It works particularly well when I use the NordicTrack. Arms, legs, breath in rhythm; body and mind one.

The Buddha sat under a tree and attained enlightenment. He didn't do walking meditation, why should I?
We don't know that for certain, do we? His sitting under the Bodhi tree was the culmination of six years of arduous ascetic practice that probably included moving from one location to another. We tend to think that the Buddha rejected his asceticism

as not being the middle way, the path to freedom. However, I wonder if instead of those six years of difficult practice, he had immediately sat under the tree, what would have been the result? The law of cause and effect (because of *this*, *that* occurs) seems to support the conclusion that the Buddha's enlightenment was a result not only of his six years in the forest, but of many lifetimes during which he purified himself.

During that first retreat when I found slow walking for long periods so difficult, my meditation deepened considerably. I, too, believed that only by sitting on my cushion could my practice ripen. One day I was filled with the desire to go outside. It was cool, sunny, and breezy—no nasty black flies about. I was torn—perhaps if I went to sit in the meditation hall, this would be the moment that I would attain enlightenment; but every cell in my body cried to be outdoors.

As I entered the woods, a glistening new world was revealed to me. I saw each individual fern, pine needle, and tuft of moss, but also was able to take in the whole. Unity and diversity. I was filled with such boundless joy and energy that I began to run along the woodland path until my energy was spent. If I hadn't had the option of walking meditation, I would have missed that revealing moment, and most surprising to me, my concentration was still strong when I returned to the meditation hall.

Everything counts. Every moment is important. Sitting, standing, walking, lying down. Staying in the present moment, without attachment or aversion or expectation is already the enlightened state.

I like to take long brisk walks. How can I keep my concentration steady?
Counting your steps is one way of focusing your attention. If you are taking a long walk, you can make the practice more challenging by counting in this manner. Beginning with your right foot, count each step up to ten; then return to one, this time counting only up to nine. Start at one and go up to eight, then move on to seven, for example:

1, 2, 3, 4, 5, 6, 7
1, 2, 3, 4, 5, 6
1, 2, 3, 4, 5
1, 2, 3, 4
1, 2, 3
1, 2
1

Then begin by counting up to ten again. It's not as easy as it seems. Whenever you notice you've lost count, return to the first sequence of one to ten.

Is there some way that I can walk outdoors at a medium pace, maintain my concentration, but still enjoy the environment?

Thich Nhat Hanh has taken elements from various traditions and created a new form of walking meditation. It can be done alone or with others. The story at the beginning of this chapter shows how it worked with emotionally disadvantaged adults. It works for everyone.

Choose a place to walk that is relatively flat and secluded. Most of us prefer to walk in the woods or at the seashore, but even the roof of an apartment building is fine. Take a couple of deep breaths and then take your first step. Imagine that you have been away from home for a long time, traveling on an ocean liner. When you reach the shore, notice the feeling of gratitude that arises as your foot touches dry land for the first time in many months. Take each step as if it were that first step. Keep the experience of each step as being new and fresh.

To maintain your concentration, you can count your steps and coordinate them with your breathing. Figure out how many steps you take on the in-breath and how many on the out-breath. For most of us, it will be uneven, for example 1-2 (in-breath), 1-2-3 (out-breath). It takes a while to get the hang of it, but it's a fine way of walking. If anything enters your awareness (a flower or rock or animal), stop and take two or three mindful breaths while you appreciate the object of your attention. Then let it go and continue walking.

I teach this method of walking to people who are HIV positive, to small children, to psychiatric patients, and just about anyone. A friend has taught it to environmentalists on a nature trail. The quiet attention needed to coordinate breath and steps opens a space where awareness sharpens and we are more likely to notice, to really see and appreciate the wonders around us. Mindful walking has a natural dignity about it that becomes respect for the environment in which we are walking.

If you'd like to slow down a bit, inhale as you lift your foot and exhale when you put it down. Take small steps, keeping your feet underneath your body. Lift—inhale; step—exhale.

I am confined to a wheelchair, so when others do walking meditation I feel left out.

There are two ways to deal with this. The first is to note the feelings that being left out triggers. There can be anger, resentment, and sadness at not being able to walk. Notice where in your body the feeling is strongest and place your full attention there, watching it wax and wane, noticing its texture, weight, and qualities. Is it concentrated or diffuse? Is it sharp or dull? Is it pleasant or unpleasant? The difficult feelings offer a way to deepen practice.

Being left out, not belonging, and being different all raise another painful emotion—separation. We can feel isolated from others because we focus on the differences instead of what we have in common. It is possible to find a walking buddy. She can practice walking where you can clearly see her. Place your attention on your buddy's steps, noting "stepping, stepping, stepping." If she walks at a consistent pace, it may be possible for you to coordinate your breath with the steps. Or silently say your mantra each time she takes a step. In addition to being able to practice walking meditation, you'll find that a bond develops between you and your walking buddy, and you won't feel quite so isolated.

Two participants during a retreat for women who are HIV positive were not able to take part in the yoga stretching before lunch. Joan had a tracheotomy and carried around her oxygen and suctioning equipment; Ricki was wearing her best clothes and didn't want to lie on the grass and get them dirty. They sat together watching the yoga class. Joan got involved and really wanted to do as much as she could. She asked Ricki to help her. Ricki began to pay attention to the instructor and helped Joan move her arms and lie down, so both became connected to the group.

Making the Practice Your Own

The Labyrinth

Many cultures and religions have a tradition of walking as spiritual practice. One that is especially conducive to meditative walking is the labyrinth. Most of us have read about the labyrinth of Crete, home of the Minotaur, but remnants of grass or stone labyrinths have been found in Western countries as well. Labyrinths were built into the marble or stone floors of cathedrals in France and today they are being constructed in Christian churches, monasteries, and convents throughout America. Some hospitals and stress clinics are also installing labyrinths.

Labyrinths are not puzzles like mazes. There are no cul-de-sacs or dead ends. There is only one route to the center. It may take twenty minutes or an hour to walk a labyrinth. The journey mirrors our life's search for serenity, ultimate truth, and freedom. Reaching the center, we reach our own center as well as the center of the universe. When we reach the center, we must complete the journey by following the path back to our everyday lives, taking with us what we have learned, incorporating it into our daily activities.

❖ Try to find a labyrinth in your area (one Web site is www.gracecathedral.org) and visit it, using the slow method of mindful walking, noting "lifting, moving, placing" or coordinating your breath with your steps.

- ◇ If you have access to a large meadow or lawn, mow your own labyrinth.

- ◇ Get together with a few friends and use masking tape to create a temporary labyrinth on the floor. Invite people to walk with you.

- ◇ Your feet can walk a labyrinth, but your hands can create one. Take a large sheet of paper, a compass, pencil, and crayon or marker. Draw concentric circles using the compass, making a template or have an oversized copy made of this pattern.

Or, design a simpler labyrinth. Follow the path with your crayon or marker, carefully moving your crayon to the center, allowing your breathing to slow down. Then choose another color crayon and retrace your "steps" to exit the labyrinth.

Medicine Walk

During a difficult spring I decided to perform a vision quest in the Sangre de Christo Mountains in Colorado. I attacked the quest as I did triathlon training—doing the reading, writing and reflection suggested.

In preparation for a vision quest, Native Americans performed a medicine walk about a month before the date of their quest. They walked from sunrise to sunset while fasting, with nothing special in mind except walking. During the walk, they would find something that would be a harbinger of what would be learned on the quest.

I decide to go to Mashomack Nature Reserve on Shelter Island, a beautiful area nestled between the north and south forks of Long Island. It feels right—the park is closed on Wednesdays and the ranger has agreed to allow me to walk the park.

The day before the walk, Hurricane Carol hits—power lines are down and the park is closed because trails are blocked by fallen trees. I wait a day or two and decide to walk from Amagansett towards Montauk. I begin at sunrise at Indian Wells beach and end there as well. I'll be able to walk along the ocean for a while, then swing over to back roads where there is not much traffic.

The first few hours are fine, but my resolve flags as the sun is nearly overhead at eleven A.M. and I'm on a quiet road bordering Napeague Harbor—a lovely view, but no shade. When I stop for water, a flashing in the brush catches my eye. It is a hunk of silver plastic—the letters RA, clearly broken off a truck like my own, a RAM. Could this be my talisman? I decide to leave it there. A few minutes later I find a single wing from a monarch butterfly. This seems trite, but as least it's symbolic. I take it with me.

By two o'clock I'm exhausted and bored. I take longer breaks and try to follow my breath. Finally, it is 5 P.M. I've been walking since 6:05 in the morning; my neck is sunburned and there are blisters on my heels. Sunset is at 7:40 and I'm concerned that I won't be able to finish before dark.

Then suddenly, I am almost in Amagansett and have to walk in a large circle to fill in the time. I reach the beach where I started a little after 6:30. I lie on the sand waiting for sunset, waiting for release—to be able to take a shower, drink as much water as I can, and eat something. And after twelve hours of walking I feel guilty because I didn't walk for another hour.

The walk has been tiring, but I am elated to have completed my task. In retrospect, the silver RA fragment seems important; I retrace my route by car to retrieve it and also to check how many miles I covered—a bit more than 23, not quite the marathon distance.

After several days the meaning of RA becomes clear—Right Attitude. This will be the theme for my quest—to keep an open mind, without judging, doing what I am told.

⋄ When you are going through a difficult time, plan your own medicine walk. Depending on your physical condition, choose to walk from sunrise to sunset or five hours or three. Once you make up your mind, determine to complete your walk no matter what. Choose to walk in a natural environment in the country or in the mountains or at the shore, anywhere you are not likely to meet many people or have to deal with cars. Bring enough water, but try to fast. During this walk, enjoy your surroundings; the focus will be on keeping a flexible mind and opening to whatever presents itself.

The answer to difficult times is always available; we just have to pay attention in order to recognize it. Notice that, like the labyrinth, we'll be walking in a rough circle, ending where we began.

Pilgrimage

The three wise men traveled to honor the Christ Child; Muslims undertake at least one *hadj* to Mecca; Japanese circle the island of Shikoku to visit all the temples; and thousands of pilgrims visit Lourdes each year. When I was a child, people would visit seven churches on Holy Thursday. Throughout history, pilgrimage has been an important spiritual practice. People undertake difficult journeys to visit sacred sites both to honor their god and to pray for a boon or miracle.

Implied in the practice of pilgrimage is difficulty—obstacles to be overcome. We have no control over the elements—it may rain or snow; roads become slick or muddy or dusty; the sun beats down on our heads or the wind works against us like a raised hand, pushing us back—no entry here. But still we carry on because we have made a vow to make the journey.

In 1961 while I was a Peace Corps volunteer in Ethiopia, one of my Ethiopian friends mentioned an annual pilgrimage to a tiny church dedicated to the Virgin Mary in the mountains at Kolubi. Childless women, accompanied by relatives, walked from their homes to Kolubi, believing that on this special feast day the Virgin there would make them fertile. For some the journey would be hundreds of miles. My friend's relatives would make the trek and he invited me to come along.

Times had changed; no longer did well-to-do women walk hundreds of miles—this family would fly into Dire Dawa and then walk the fifteen or so miles through the mountains at night, hoping to arrive at Kolubi at dawn, the most auspicious time.

We were a band of about nine, with a local man who would guide us through the mountains. Although the terrain would be rocky and rough and we had only flashlights to guide our way, I was amazed to see that the women were wearing their ordinary street clothes and the flimsy ballet-like slippers that were de rigueur among Ethiopian women. One man carried an enormous picnic cooler filled with food and wine—I was the only one who carried a container of water.

We set out before dusk and the group was jubilant. Only as it darkened and the flat road became hilly and rock-strewn did the mood quiet down. Finally it had dawned that this would be no walk in the park. The climbs in pitch dark would be dangerous, and we had mosquitoes, snakes, and hyenas to worry about. *Shiftas* (wandering bandits) abounded in the area. It was rumored that the last remaining black-maned lions in Ethiopia ranged these hills.

We slogged on. Batteries wore out. A woman began to weep. Although I was wearing heavy walking shoes, I began to get blisters, and my arms were scratched by brush at the side of the trail. What trail? We had placed our trust in a now-drunk stranger to lead us the correct way.

When we finally crawled over the last ridge, we could see the sun rise behind the church. The valley was filled with hundreds of other pilgrims, with one side of the vale covered by seated women wearing their native *shamas,* skirts ballooned out like a thousand white blossoms on the side of the hill. Later I discovered that this was the women's toilet area.

All the hardship was forgotten in the elation of having reached the church. We attended the outdoor Coptic Christian service, women who hoped to conceive healthy babies made offerings, and after feasting we began our return journey—this time by car on a paved road. It took forty minutes.

There's something magical about hardship. Even people who are not religious seek it out. Today, we run marathons and ultra-marathons, climb Himalayan mountains, and compete against ourselves in the Iron Man triathlon or Eco-Challenge.

Although it may not be voiced or understood, there is the imperative to search for something. There is the need to see what we are made of, and in enduring a long trek or pilgrimage or race the danger dumps us squarely in the present moment. We are too exhausted to plan the future; we just take one step at a time, "stepping, stepping, stepping." That's all there is and we reach a place of serenity. We are in the meditative state.

⋄ Choose a place that is important to you in some way. It may be your grandmother's home, a religious site, a relative's grave, or a spiritual teacher giving a lecture. You may have a favorite outdoor spot that brings you peace. Make a vow to walk there.

⋄ Nowadays there are many walkathons and bike-athons to raise money for good causes. Choose a cause that is meaningful to you and join up; this can be your pilgrimage.

⋄ Many have marched to show support for racial, religious, or sexual equality or to preserve the environment or to protest war, nuclear testing, land mines. The next time there is a march for something you believe in strongly, join it. This can be your pilgrimage. Leave behind any anger and resentment, and concentrate on taking each step mindfully. When the Buddha was born he took eight steps and in each footprint a lotus bloomed. As you take each step, imagine a flower blooming in your footprint.

Bowing

Many Buddhists make a pilgrimage to Mount Kailas in Tibet. Most simply walk around the base of the mountain, but some make a full prostration with each step. In Eastern traditions bowing is an extension of walking mediation. The whole body is used in each prostration, and selfish desires and thoughts are erased. Some Tibetan practitioners vow to make ten thousand bows to purify the mind/heart and bring one to a place of no-thought.

Westerners find it difficult to bend our backs (and our wills) to another. I, too, resisted bowing. Only when I broke down the motions was I able to approach it the same way as walking meditation. When we bow, we are not bowing to a particular person or being. We simply join our body and minds, as we join our palms, being present in the bowing.

Exercise

To make a standing bow, place your hands palms together in front of your face, with the tips of the fingers about nose height. This is called *gassho*. Stand erect and bow from the waist.

To make a full prostration, start in the position for standing bow. As your hands come down, begin to lower your knees. When your knees and head are touching the earth, move your hands apart, palms facing the sky and raise them slightly. This symbolizes turning over your life and death to a power greater than yourself (God, Buddha, Christ, Allah, the Source). You are surrendering your small self to your greater self and in so doing you are releasing your burdens. Your open hands are letting go of anger, sadness, and fear. By surrendering your will, you become free. Rise to your feet slowly, using a hand to help lift yourself if necessary; return to standing bow position and finish by bowing from the waist.

When I was ordained as a monk, I entered the zendo and was instructed to make three bows to the Buddha, my teacher, and my parents. When I made a full prostration in front of my mother, she burst into tears and so did I. I had never expressed my appreciation to my parents in such a visceral way. Birthday presents and Mother's Day cards were superficial and had not acknowledged the depth of my gratitude to her. In fact, I had forgotten that I owed her anything for her love, protection, and understanding throughout the ups and downs of my life.

Now, whenever I perform a wedding ceremony, I ask the bride and groom to make a standing bow in gratitude to their parents for giving them life and nurturing them. Invariably, even parents who are leery of attending a Buddhist ceremony are touched.

- The next time you see your parents, make a standing bow to them.

- Try making a bow each morning to express gratitude for the new day or each evening to show your appreciation for having lived another day.

- When you see something awe-inspiring or beautiful, make a standing bow to express your appreciation.

- Each time you sit down to meditate, bow to your chair or cushion.

- Try bowing your head before eating a meal.

- When you feel overwhelmed by grief or sorrow or fear, make a full prostration to surrender your problems to a higher power.

Work Practice

A student asked his meditation teacher, "What is your spiritual practice?"

The teacher responded, "I chop wood and carry water."

At many Buddhist retreats, work practice is an integral part of the daily schedule. You carry the mindfulness gained in sitting and walking meditation into activities such as mowing the lawn, vacuuming, and washing dishes. When you are in a quiet state of mind, everything can be practice.

Connie's seatmate on the bus to a Zen retreat was a Tibetan monk who was fingering his mala. He explained to Connie that he used it to count mantras and calm his mind. During her retreat, Connie's work practice was helping to get out a large mailing of newsletters. Her job was to remove a name sticker from a strip, place it on the front of the newsletter, then turn the newsletter over so that when stacked the names would remain in alphabetical order. She did this for a whole week. At first she was bored, but gradually she found a rhythm in lifting a sticker, placing it on a newsletter, then turning it over—"lifting, placing, turning." Connie had found a way to make this job her meditation and she realized that the newsletters had become her mala.

- ◆ Choose a household task that you do everyday. Make this your meditation by focusing on the repetitive actions. Pulling weeds, dusting, sweeping, raking leaves are good beginnings.

- ◆ Choose a chore that you find tedious and make it a ritual, like the tea ceremony. I loved windsurfing, but had an aversion to rigging up and, especially after a tiring day, rigging down to go home. I placed my full attention on unlocking the masthead, sliding the mast from the sail, rinsing the sail, and furling it loosely. Then I'd make three trips to the car carrying the board, the mast and boom, and finally the sail, and lifting them onto the roof rack. "Unlocking, sliding, rinsing, furling, carrying, lifting." One day, as I was derigging I noticed some people had gathered to watch. The ritual had become a rhythmic, calming spectacle.

- ◆ If you are engaged in work that is frantic or stressful, resolve to take a mini-break every hour, by stopping and mindfully watching your breath going in and out at least three times. Then return to work.

Play Practice

Lately there have been news articles and books about the meditative state that can be achieved in sports. Players talk about being "in the zone," a place where time slows down and everything flows. A home-run hitter sees the ball approach his bat as surely as a nail to a magnet. A basketball player knows the second he releases it that the ball will enter the hoop. A skater executes a triple axel effortlessly. They have become one with the present moment and have left thinking behind. The perfect pitch or shot happens automatically without planning or worrying. Instinct takes over.

But those transcendent moments are preceded by years of practice and occur rarely.

- The next time you participate in an athletic activity, psych yourself *down* by taking several deep breaths. Notice your surroundings. For example, if you're planning to swim notice the sensation of the cool water as you slide in. Notice how it envelops you like a placenta. Feel yourself move through it. Notice how you become part of the water.

- When you warm up for your sport, try to follow your breaths while you stretch.

- Connect with your body by taking t'ai chi, tae kwon do, or qi gong lessons.

- Take a class in tap dancing.

Eating Practice

At some retreats there is a ritual for eating called *oryoki*. Each person has a set of three nested bowls wrapped in a cloth that is used as a place mat. The bundle includes utensils, a napkin, and a dishcloth. While the bundle is being unwrapped, the bowls arranged on the placemat, and the food served, the retreatants chant. Here is part of it:

> Thus we eat this food with everyone,
> We eat to stop all evil,
> To practice good,
> To save all sentient beings,
> And to accomplish the Enlightened Way.

The ritual of receiving food, eating it mindfully, and cleaning our bowls thoroughly keeps us in the present moment. We pay attention to each part of the meal—the cleaning and wrapping of the bowls is no less important than the eating of food. It is practice just as walking and breathing are practice. Our day becomes seamless; there is no difference between sitting meditation and the rest of our activities.

- Choose one meal to practice mindfulness of eating. Set your place carefully, and when you are ready to eat, notice the taste, texture, and color of the food. Feel the warmth or coolness as it reaches your mouth. After you've finished eating, wash and dry your dishes carefully and store them in their proper place. Express your gratitude before and after eating the meal.

- Create your own chant or invocation or prayer to recite silently before you eat.

- Reflect on your other daily routines. Can you perform them mindfully, instead of mindlessly? Create invocations for bathing, brushing your teeth, waking up, going to sleep.

Walking, working, playing, eating. Every activity can be a meditation. All we have to do is be mindful of what is happening in the present moment and we'll discover well-being and serenity.

Five

Opening the Heart

METTA (LOVING-KINDNESS) PRACTICES

Ben has a brain tumor and is in the end stages of AIDS. A couple of days before my visit he has suffered a seizure and lost his ability to speak. He is terrified of having another seizure and losing his ability to communicate. As we talk, Ben's head begins to jerk, his body spasms, eyes roll, and he opens his mouth in an almost silent scream. He is having another seizure.

For a second I freeze, then call the nurse; the code team arrives to help Ben. It takes only several minutes to stabilize him, and then we are alone again. Ben's nightmare has become a reality—he is not able to speak. The terror in the room is palpable. I am frightened, too—my mouth dry and my stomach like a clenched fist. His eyes are begging for something, but I have no words for him.

In that moment of not-knowing, I begin stroking his head and repeating the metta phrases.

May you be safe from harm.
May you be happy and peaceful.
May you be strong and healthy.
May you be free from suffering.

I repeat the phrases over and over, as much for myself as for Ben. Gradually the atmosphere in the room changes—instead of being charged with tension and filled with darkness, it seems to soften and brighten. Ben relaxes into sleep, and I am filled with a peace and acceptance and joy that I have never experienced before. In offering loving-kindness to another, I am being healed myself.

When Ben awakens, he is able to raise his arms to me asking for a hug, and as I cradle his wasted body, we are connected in a very intimate way. There is no separation; his heartbeat is my heartbeat; his pain, my pain; his life and death, mine. Metta has created a space where fear has been transformed into unconditional love.

During my second year of chaplaincy training, I sometimes listened to a guided metta meditation tape during the long commute to the hospital. I began to notice that when I practiced metta the quality of my day improved. Patients were more forthcoming with their problems, and I was able to open to their suffering without bursting into tears or distancing myself by erecting a glass wall between us. The bone-numbing exhaustion I normally felt after a twelve-hour day lessened. But I did not attempt using metta with patients until I met Ben.

I have used metta with cancer and AIDS patients, emotionally and mentally retarded adults, battered women; in a psychiatric ward and a detox unit; for professional caregivers in danger of burnout, persons with Multiple Personality and Dissociative Disorder, teen-aged substance abusers at a rehab; and with my own sister when she was dying. People respond to metta practice no matter what their personal beliefs. Everyone needs loving-kindness.

The Buddha taught that the twin fruits of meditation are wisdom and compassion. They are like the wings of a bird: lacking one, the bird cannot fly. Mindfulness and koan practices focus on arousing wisdom, but wisdom is not enough; we need compassion to balance our lives.

There is a path of practice called the *brahma viharas* (divine abodes) to help us uncover and nurture the qualities of compassion and to bring balance to our lives. Elements of the viharas are *metta* (loving-kindness), *karuna* (compassion), *mudita* (sympathetic joy), and *upekkha* (equanimity).

When practicing the divine abodes, we always begin with metta, for loving-kindness is the foundation on which the others are built. It is taught that one who practices metta meditation sleeps peacefully, has pleasant dreams, is loved by humans and animals, is protected by celestial beings, is safe from danger, has a joyful mind, has a bright and serene visage, dies peacefully, and has a fortunate rebirth. Sounds good to me!

◾

SENDING METTA TO OURSELVES

In working with metta, we begin with ourselves, then radiate the loving-kindness to a benefactor or mentor, a dear friend, a neutral person, and then a difficult person. Eventually we can include all the people, animals, and nature around us, as well as the entire universe.

But we start with ourselves. If we cannot love and accept ourselves exactly as we are, how can we expect to love others?

To practice metta, begin by sitting in one of the meditation postures—on a cushion, on a chair, or in bed. Since we are learning to be kind to ourselves, if you experience extreme discomfort, it's okay to change your position. It is helpful to close your eyes, but if that is uncomfortable for you, gaze at the floor at a forty-five-degree angle with unfocused eyes.

Visualize yourself as the object of metta. You can use a picture of yourself as you are now or at another time in your life—perhaps when you were a baby or a child. If visualization is difficult for you, then say your name occasionally during the meditation. It is important to connect with yourself as the object of metta.

We'll be working with four phrases that have been translated and adapted from the Pali language. The phrases I have found that work well for those who are ill or emotionally distressed are:

May I be safe from inner and outer harm.
May I be happy and peaceful.
May I be strong and healthy.
May I take care of myself with joy.

As always, the breath will be our anchor. When your mind wanders, or when you're distracted by sound, return to the sensation of your breath going in and out, and repeat the phrases silently to yourself. To connect in a visceral way to yourself as the object of metta and to relax your body if you are tense or anxious, begin with a body scan. You can do this for yourself or guide a friend. As you go through the meditation, leave enough time between the instructions to notice the movement of relaxation, and go slowly. During the silence between the phrases, focus on your breath.

Guided Meditation

Sit or lie in a position that you can hold comfortably. Close your eyes if you like and take a couple of really deep breaths, feeling your breath going in and out and noticing your chest rising and falling.

Now bring your attention to the top of your head and wish your head well.

May my mind be clear and spacious like the sky, may all negative thoughts and feelings and memories drift away like clouds.

May my mind be filled with ease, well-being, and serenity.

Imagine the feeling of well-being moving down your face—around your eyes, your nose, your cheeks, and mouth, so that all the muscles of your face begin to soften and relax.

Imagine the well-being moving into your jaw, down your neck, across your shoulders, down your arms, and into your hands and fingers, so that the top part of your body feels light and easy.

Let the relaxation flow down your back, vertebra by vertebra, washing away any tightness or tension.

Feel the relaxation radiate through your chest, around your

heart, in your stomach so that all knots are untied and everything is soft and easy.

Let the well-being move through your hips, down your legs, into your feet and toes.

Take a moment to enjoy all the muscles of your body working together in harmony, with no tightness and no tension.

Take a couple of really deep breaths, being aware of your breath going in and out, feeling your chest rising and falling.

I ask you to visualize yourself as you are now or at some other time in your life. Take the image of yourself, place it in your heart, and surround it with care and tenderness.

> May I be safe from inner and outer harm.
> May I be happy and peaceful.
> May I be strong and healthy.
> May I take care of myself with joy.

The words aren't important; it's the meaning behind the words—the feeling of being

> safe
> happy
> peaceful
> strong
> healthy and
> cared for

Just keep repeating the phrases, always connecting to yourself as the object of metta.

> May I be safe from harm.
> May I be happy and peaceful.
> May I be strong and healthy.
> May I take care of myself with joy.

If your mind wanders or if you're distracted by sounds, just come back to the sensation of your breath going in and out and the phrases or just the keywords:

safe
happy
peaceful
strong
healthy and
cared for

Connect with a deep wellspring of love and acceptance for yourself, exactly as you are.

May I be safe from harm.
May I be happy and peaceful.
May I be strong and healthy.
May I take care of myself with joy.

Now practice the metta on your own for a time, remembering to return to the phrases when your attention drifts.
(Practice on your own for some time)
If you'd like to, extend the loving-kindness to everyone in the room (house, building, neighborhood).

May we be safe from harm.
May we be happy and peaceful.
May we be strong and healthy.
May we take care of ourselves with joy.

When you're ready, open your eyes and come back to the room.

Did you notice a difference in the quality of loving-kindness when you sent it to other people? This reveals a lot about ourselves. For many of us, it is easier to send metta to other people and harder to feel it for ourselves. Some of us are so needy of attention that we experience resistance when we're asked to send metta to others. Just notice what is true for you, without judging. We are all connected, so when you experience loving-kindness for yourself, all beings are included. When you experience it for others, you are included.

When we look carefully at the metta phrases, we realize that they contain all we need to be truly happy. Notice that they don't mention finding a lover or getting a better job or winning the lottery.

My friend Jackie has wanted to meditate for a long time, but like most of us has put off learning how to do it. When she saw the metta phrases for the first time, she knew that they were something that she could do. As she began to work with the phrases, tears came to her eyes. A deep sadness and fear that she had masked with anger arose.

Jackie had been abused by her former husband, and by withholding financial support from her children he still maintained control over her. Working with the phrase, "May I be safe from harm," empowered Jackie. She was able to disentangle herself from the story of why she felt sad and fearful. She began to know that she deserved to be safe and came to believe that she and her children would be safe from harm. Often, when she practiced metta, she visualized herself sitting with her children enfolded in her arms.

For others, "May I be happy and peaceful" is most important.

There are five people sitting around an oilcloth-covered table in the sunroom of a county hospital. One man is clutching a coffee cup as if it's his life preserver; another leers at me, trying to assert his power by flirting. Two prostitutes are dissing each other. I recognize an older man who has been here before. Welcome to the weekly meditation meeting in detox. For me, it is the most challenging group I lead.

Because of lack of funding, people who are brought in by police or who sign themselves in are treated for five days, then sent on to a rehab or back to the streets. This is a county hospital, not a posh facility. The clients here are mostly black, poor, and homeless. Some are glad to come to detox because the streets are too cold in winter and the shelters are dangerous. No one is interested in meditation, but they must attend every lecture, AA meeting, group therapy session, and interview with counselors. Each week I meet a new group and start from scratch.

I introduce myself as a Buddhist priest and then mention that I am in recovery myself. I explain metta, do the body scan, and guide the meditation for ten minutes. A couple of people are napping, their heads lolling on the table. When I end the meditation by sounding the bells, one person literally wakes up. Another asks, "You tryin' to hypnotize me?"

I ask them what the meditation has been like for them. Silence. One woman says, "It was nice." Then I begin a discussion on the meaning of the phrases. There is a little more interaction.

The older man, who has been in and out of detox several times, looks up and wistfully says that once he and his young son took the subway to Rockaway Beach and fished off the jetty. They had a good time even though they hadn't caught any fish. He was happy then.

A younger man says he's always searching for the big score and for excitement, but he'd really like to settle down in a small house and do regular stuff—like having a barbecue in the backyard. One of the women begins to cry; she wants to get her kid out of foster care—that's why she's here to straighten herself out.

Each person has a dream, an image of what happiness would be for them. During the second ten-minute meditation, all are sitting up relatively straight, eyes closed repeating the phrases with me, "May I be happy and peaceful."

At the time I taught my first retreat for people with AIDS most patients died within a couple of years. The chaplain at the agency asked me to change one phrase to "May I be strong of heart"; she thought patients would feel bad because they would never be strong and healthy. I agreed to do this, deciding that doing the retreat was the paramount objective. After all, these people needed courage to face their end.

I always print the phrases on slips of paper that I hand out to retreatants. This day, I took the "wrong" handouts. As it turned out, "May I be strong and healthy" was the most meaningful phrase for the participants. Hope was as important as courage, and with new treatments, people with HIV are living ten or twenty years in good health. Now they are called people living with HIV, and cancer patients are cancer survivors.

It is particularly with cancer patients that "May I take care of myself with joy" seems to resonate. Imagine undergoing MRIs, biopsies, surgery, chemotherapy, radiation. Imagine doing so joyfully. It's possible.

When Judy was diagnosed with cancer she shaved her head, leaving a small tuft in front, which she dyed lavender. Each fingernail was painted a different color, and she got her first tattoo. She attended many programs at the cancer support center and began to write about her cancer. Judy began to take care of herself joyfully.

Often people attend workshops or retreats and find metta practice too flowery. Longtime meditators are resistant, as I was. They get so attached to their own practice that they begin to think other practices are not important.

I taught a metta retreat at a Zen center and the resistance in the room was palpable. Many students had been practicing in the same way for years. At the end of the day, some people had opened to metta, but the majority had drifted back to their own practice.

Several weeks later, I received a letter from one of the students. During a long bike trip through the mountains, he became negative about the journey—the backpack was too heavy, the hills too steep, the day too hot. Then he began to visualize himself as a child and repeated the metta phrases during the rest of the journey. He said that the wholesome thoughts of metta nurtured him and helped him through his journey. The practice also gave him insight into some of his personal patterns of negativity.

Metta works. We may not experience an epiphany while sitting on the cushion, but metta slowly but surely transforms the way we relate to the world and ourselves. We begin to befriend ourselves, and the feeling of well-being extends to those around us.

Going Deeper

I have trouble remembering the phrases.

Don't worry about it. Repeat the phrases that you *do* remember or just use three or four keywords—safe, happy, peaceful, healthy.

I'm going along nicely and then I notice that I'm mixing the words up—May I be happy and healthy or May I be peaceful and strong.

You might have stumbled on a phrase that is more meaningful to you, or perhaps you're losing concentration and drifting. As soon as you notice that you are not mindful of the phrases, note "drifting," and begin saying the phrases (silently) with more energy, placing emphasis on each word.

All of a sudden I realize that a different phrase has popped into my mind. Is this okay?

Yes, there may be a special area that needs attention. I attended my first ten-day metta retreat hoping to learn to do metta so that I could help my patients, but by the second day I realized that I needed to do it for myself, and the phrases that were suggested to me were: "May I love myself exactly as I am" and "May I be happy with things just as they are." I worked with those phrases, and I found that my relationship to myself shifted and I became less judgmental. As I began to accept myself, I was less harsh in my judgments of others.

When I say the phrases, it seems like I'm asking God to help me. Metta feels like a prayer.

The purpose of practicing metta is to soften ourselves so that we're ready to let go of fear, unhappiness, and other harmful emotions to make space for a feeling of well-being. When I work with people from various faith traditions, I encourage them to adapt the practice in any way that is meaningful to them. If this means using metta like a prayer, that's okay.

When I visited a friend who was hospitalized, he told me this story:

Bob had been introduced to metta practice a few years ago and used it often, working with the phrases: "May I be safe from harm," "May I be happy and peaceful," "May I be strong and healthy," "May I be free." When he traveled to a large medical center for a week of tests to determine if he had colon cancer, he experienced nervousness. Two of the procedures were particularly anxiety-producing. One was a cardiac stress test involving a radioactive substance and the other was a second biopsy.

While he waited for the tests he did metta mindfully, like a prayer, using the phrases that helped him when he felt in danger. It occurred to him to change the last phrase to "May I be free from fear." After an hour or so he sensed a being of light behind him, larger than life, with its wings folded protectively around him. He felt enveloped in a soft, benevolent light. Quick as an exhalation, the anxiety disappeared, replaced by a sudden calm. He underwent the tests with little nervousness, knowing that all would be well.

I get confused and don't know whether to focus on my breath or the phrases.

The breath is in the background during this meditation—repeating the phrases like a mantra is important to connect to loving-kindness. When you notice that your mind is drifting, come back to the feeling of the breath, connect with yourself, and then begin to repeat the phrases. Sometimes it helps to switch to the key words and match them to your exhalation. For example, exhale (safe), exhale (happy), exhale (peaceful). Choose three or four of the key-words and keep repeating them, connecting with yourself.

When I repeat the phrases I get angry and resentful because I'm not happy and peaceful and I don't think I ever have been.

Metta is a purification practice. Sometimes our pain is so deep that it's necessary to address it before we can feel tenderness for ourselves. As with a rotten molar, the decay has to be removed before the tooth can be filled with gold. We have to fully acknowledge and accept our difficult emotions before we can transform them.

I felt so terrific after my first metta retreat that I returned the next year for three weeks expecting to experience love, connectedness, and bliss. But I couldn't arouse loving-kindness for anyone or anything, even my dog that I love dearly.

My work practice at the retreat was preparing salad for lunch, and as I repeated the phrases silently to myself, I vented my anger by tearing the lettuce to shreds. May I be safe from harm. RIP! May I be happy and peaceful. RIP! Although the retreat was not as joyful and serene as I had hoped, afterwards I noticed that my lifelong repressed anger and depression had abated and my relationships with other people improved. Healing had begun.

I can't feel any love for myself. I just feel flat.
Just because you don't feel love during one meditation session doesn't mean that you'll never experience it. Conversely, even if you experience an epiphany, don't expect that it will occur each time you meditate. Everything changes. Metta helps us to open to what is, right now, at this moment; experience it fully and embrace it.

Try thinking of someone for whom you do feel unconditional love—small children or grandchildren or pets are good for this. Send the metta to them and when you start to feel the love well up, quickly switch back to yourself. When the caring feeling fades, switch back to your loved one. Another tactic is to imagine being with the other person (your child, for example). Change the phrases accordingly, "May *we* be safe from harm."

If the aversion is very strong and interferes with the metta practice, then attend with mindfulness to the sensation in your body that accompanies the aversion. Notice where in the body it appears. Is it widespread or concentrated? Is it soft or hard? Is it dark or light? Avoid getting caught up in the story of *why* you feel aversion. Try to stay with the sensation in the body. As it lessens, return to metta.

What should loving-kindness feel like during the meditation?

It's different for everyone. Some people experience overwhelming joy and connectedness; others feel a sense of well-being and warmth. For some tears well up. For some the body relaxes, and it's as if the walls they've built to protect themselves are beginning to crumble and the heart/mind is opening. Sometimes it's painful because we're not used to being vulnerable and open.

For several months I led a metta meditation session at the in-patient psychiatric ward of a county hospital. I had met with the department head and we agreed to use the following phrases:

May I be happy.
May I be peaceful.
May my heart be free from pain.

Since several patients were schizophrenic, it was important to replace the negative voices in their heads with positive messages. There were also people suffering from drug/alcohol abuse, manic-depression, and mental retardation. How would they respond?

I began with the guided body scan and kept each meditation period only ten minutes long. In between we discussed the meaning of the phrases and what had come up for the members of the group.

Sometimes it seemed as if nothing happened during the sessions. Some participants were non-committal and others napped, but some responded. A woman who had been to four meetings told me she would be released the next day. She asked me for all the slips of paper with the phrases written on them to give to her college friends.

A young girl told me she had "lots of bad feelings inside," but could not cry and hoped the phrases would help her. Another told me she heard voices telling her to hurt herself (she had cut her arms with razor blades and sometimes burned herself with a cigarette butt). I suggested she use the phrase, "May I be safe from harm."

A suicidal alcoholic started crying quietly and told me she could not remember a time in her life when she had been happy. In spite of her sadness, she stayed for the second meditation period and at the end her tears were gone, replaced by a radiant smile. She had remembered a time when she had been happy—at a rehab where she had been given a birthday party and had felt surrounded by love. Metta had unlocked a beautiful memory that could sustain her during difficult times.

One evening, at the end of the second period when I suggested that the group extend loving-kindness to the person sitting beside them, Peter, a slightly retarded schizophrenic, touched the hand of his neighbor. One by one people grasped hands in a chain reaction. The meditation ended with these isolated, forgotten people joined in a circle of love and connectedness. For once they belonged.

What's the difference between the metta phrases and affirmations? Can I say, "I am happy and peaceful"?

When we practice metta, we are acknowledging and accepting where we are right now, but opening ourselves to the possibility of change. The words "May I" have a vulnerable, caring quality that imply that we deserve to be happy and peaceful. In a sense, we are willing to be willing to accept happiness and peace. But when we say, "I am happy and peaceful," it may not be true. Affirmations tend to deny our true feelings of unworthiness and have a demanding quality. We don't like something and we want it to change immediately.

I experience a deep feeling of peace but I'm not sure that it's really loving-kindness.

That's a good observation. Since metta is a concentration practice, it helps develop samadhi and it's possible to mistake the pleasant sensations that arise at deeper levels of meditation for loving-kindness. Connect with the phrases with more energy and try an experiment: Attempt sending the metta to a difficult person and check the quality of the feeling.

I repeat the phrases over and over, then I notice a feeling of warmth and peace, and the words fall away. Is this all right?
Yes. Remember it's the meaning behind the words, not the words themselves that are important. Just rest in the feeling that arises. When it fades, or when your mind wanders, return to the phrases.

Making the Practice Your Own

⋄ Look at each of the metta phrases and discover what each one means for you.

⋄ At this particular time in your life, which phrase is most meaningful for you? Why? If your meaningful phrase is "May I be safe from harm," capture the feeling of harm or danger by drawing or painting what harm means to you. What color is it? What shape does it have? Is it large or small? Is it abstract or recognizable? Then write down all the words that come into your mind when you think of harm or danger. Can you write a poem using those words?

⋄ Take a second sheet of paper and using the same metta phrase, draw what safety means to you. Write down all the words that relate to being safe. If you wish, write a poem or story using those words.

⋄ Try walking meditation to deepen metta. The focus will be on the phrases and your stepping. Walk at a medium or slow pace, placing your foot on the ground as you say each phrase silently. After a time, you may wish to switch to just four of the keywords, whichever are most important to you. When your attention wanders, stop; take a couple of deep breaths to refocus yourself and then continue walking while silently saying the phrases or keywords.

- ❖ When you are traveling on a bus or train, practice the phrases while fingering a mala.

SENDING METTA TO OTHERS

When the feeling of loving-kindness arises, it will fill your cup and begin to overflow, and the desire to include other people will arise. At first choose someone for whom it is easy to arouse metta. In Eastern countries many people have a benefactor or mentor (for example, a spiritual teacher).

If you don't have a mentor, choose a child, grandchild, or favorite grandparent. Since we are trying to arouse the feeling of loving-kindness, it is not suggested to use your mate as an object—for although there may be love and mutual respect, there can also be some residual resentment from disagreements and arguments. It is better not to choose someone who is very ill or dead, because there is usually an undercurrent of sadness that tinges the meditation. Try someone easy at first.

Guided Meditation

Begin by sending metta to yourself. After some time, when you feel centered and the feeling of care is strong, visualize the other person, place her in your heart, and surround her with care and tenderness.

As I wish myself to be safe from harm, so I wish you to be safe.

> May you be happy and peaceful.
> May you be strong and healthy.
> May you take care of yourself with joy.

Sometimes it's difficult to feel loving-kindness for another, so it's helpful to do the forgiveness practice:

> For all the harm I have done to others, knowingly or
> unknowingly; forgive me.

For all the harm others have done to me knowingly or
    unknowingly; I forgive you as much as I can.
For all the harm I have done to myself, knowingly or
    unknowingly; I forgive myself.
May you be safe from harm.
May you be happy and peaceful.
May you be strong and healthy.
May you take care of yourself with joy.

(Continue for some time, always connecting with the other person as the object of metta.)
    When you're ready, open your eyes and come back to the room.

After you've practiced sending metta to a benefactor, then try a dear
friend. When you're ready, move on to a neutral person. When you
think that your heart is bursting with love and acceptance, try sending it to a difficult person. Just dip your toes in to test the water—
if you're not ready to let go of anger and resentment, simply say,
"not now," and return to the neutral person.

Going Deeper

*When I'm sending metta to one person, another person needing loving-
kindness comes into my mind. What should I do?*

Everyone needs loving-kindness, but in this meditation we're also
trying to develop our concentration powers. When another person
comes into your consciousness, say the phrases once for him, then
return to your original object. Or, you can make a conscious decision to switch to him as the primary metta object. At the end of the
sitting, you may want to include everyone in the loving-kindness.

*I'm really getting bored with saying the phrases, and I keep losing con-
nection with the metta object.*

Sometimes the practice can be dry. So we can keep our energy
up by piquing our interest. For example, you can imagine the
person wearing different clothing or in different settings. The

important thing is to keep your connection with the other person. If it is helpful, try sending metta to yourself as well: "May *we* be safe . . . ."

I start with myself, then move on to a benefactor, and then a dear friend, but they all blend together and we don't seem like separate people any more. I just feel loving-kindness.

That's fine. Rest in the feeling of loving-kindness—that's what the practice is about. When you notice that you are drifting, connect again with one of the people and the phrases.

Even though I really like the person I'm sending metta to, I keep remembering little things he did that upset me.

Wouldn't it be wonderful if no one ever upset us! Gradually as we practice loving-kindness, compassion, sympathetic joy, and equanimity we develop stability and recognize that no one upsets us but ourselves. In the meantime, try the forgiveness practice again. Whenever I am angry with someone, if I say the phrase, "For all the harm you have done to me, knowingly or unknowingly, I forgive you as much as I can," it feels as if a rope around my chest has been loosened and I can breathe freely again.

It may be time for you to try the metta on a neutral person— someone you don't know at all (the postman, for example) and have not made any judgments about.

At the end of one retreat, I found a note on my cushion telling me that I had been someone's neutral person. I felt terrific knowing that someone had been sending me metta for ten days. When I shared this during the retreat's closing circle, two others told me they had been sending me metta as well.

Forgiveness practice sounds good, but I have been so hurt in my life I can't imagine forgiving the person.

That's a difficult place to be. Remember that the main purpose of metta practice is to open *our own* heart to loving-kindness. The teacher who suggested that we add "as much as I can" to the end of the phrases was very wise. How many of us are able to forgive completely and let go? We do the practice so that our own heart can open and be free from suffering.

If you can say the phrases, even without feeling them, it is still setting the stage for real forgiveness later. It indicates a willing heart. But be kind to yourself. You may want to change the phrase to "I forgive you as much as I can, but not now." Letting go happens little by little—be patient with yourself.

My friend Kathy, who had suffered physical and emotional abuse, wrote to me about what forgiveness practice meant to her:

> When I first heard about forgiveness practice, a couple of things leaped out at me right away. "As much as I can" let me off the hook up front.
>
> This was the first gleam of light I'd felt in this matter for a long time. It meant I didn't have to completely or totally profess I was feeling something that, in my heart, I knew wasn't true. It meant that if the only thing I could do at that moment was to recite this practice, just get the words out of my mouth, that would be all right.
>
> "As much as I can" establishes a gray area for me, where before only black and white demarcations reigned. There need be no definites or absolutes. In the shadowy gray, a door opens, a door leading to the notion that whatever I can manage to feel at the time is sufficient. If I am striving, according to the concept of right effort, to rid myself of any evil inside me, then mere sufficiency won't do forever. But when I am in the midst of confusion and hurt brought on by human relations, I can do only so much. A little at a time is okay. When it comes to forgiveness, I definitely have to take baby steps before I can walk, and forgiveness practice is a practical way to do that.
>
> Being made to focus for a moment on "the harm I have done to others" takes the sting out of others' hurtful actions toward me. When I am guided to recall that I have

sometimes done things that can't be described as welcome, I am better prepared to understand that other people are human like me. I am sure there are many times I have hurt others, because it seems that if you live long enough, it's just bound to happen. Many times it was unknowingly, and I might think that since it was unintentional, it didn't count. Of course, that doesn't make sense when I'm on the receiving end of the slight or slash.

So, the most interesting facet of this practice is that it forces me to look at both sides at once and to stand in the other person's shoes before I put my own on.

I was sending metta to a friend and I began to experience physical desire for her.

That's why it is suggested that you not choose a mate or lover as a metta object. The near enemy of metta is desire or lust. In some ways they seem alike, but romantic love can be self-serving. Usually we want the other person to love us back or to give us what we want.

Metta is unconditional love—we love because that is our natural, undefiled state of being. We love ourselves or a friend or even an enemy without wanting anything from them or wanting them to change. We love them exactly as they are, including all their foibles and flaws. Metta practice helps us to open to what is.

Especially during longer retreats, lustful thoughts are bound to arise. We tend to forget that it's simply desire, one of the hindrances. It's just a thought—there's no need to beat yourself up about it or be drawn into a fantasy. Simply note "desire" and return to your practice. If the thoughts don't abate, switch to mindfulness practice, working with the sensation of desire, not the story.

Does metta really work? Will my brother who has cancer become strong and healthy?

Metta does work, but perhaps not in the way we want it to. The purpose of the practice is to open *our own* heart to love and compassion for others and ourselves. It helps to transform our relationship to painful physical and emotional mind states from one of denial or fear to one of acceptance and serenity.

In recent studies on the healing power of intercessory prayer and meditation, it has been found that persons who are receiving prayer and meditation are more likely to heal. To me, it is the sense of connection between human beings that prayer or meditation engenders that loosens the knots in the body and allows energy to flow. A person who is calm and relaxed instead of contracted and anxious is more likely to be receptive to medical protocols. Some people say that if you believe metta will heal, it will. I leave it you to decide which way to proceed. It may be more appropriate to do karuna (compassion) practice for someone who's ill. (see page 92)

Making the Practice Your Own

❖ When you are on a crowded bus or walking down the street, try sending metta to each person you see within a space of five minutes. Just look at each person, smile, and say silently "May you be happy." Notice any changes in your mood. A good time to practice metta is while waiting in line at the supermarket.

❖ If you are involved in a confrontation and your adversary is very angry, try saying "May you be happy" or "I wish you well" silently to yourself, before reacting. Does your adversary's stance soften? Do you still feel attacked?

❖ If you use e-mail, send a metta phrase to everyone in your address book.

❖ Try extending the loving-kindness as far as you can.

Guided Meditation

Take a couple of deep breaths and connect to your body. Feel your buttocks touching your cushion or chair.

Be aware of your knees or feet touching the floor.

As you breathe in and out, visualize yourself as you are now or at some other time in your life.

Regard yourself with deep care and affection and begin the metta phrases:

May I be safe from harm.
May I be happy and peaceful.
May I be strong and healthy.
May I take care of myself with joy.

Connect to the feeling of unconditional love for yourself while repeating the phrases silently to yourself.
(Continue for some time sending metta to yourself.)

Now include everyone in the house in the loving-kindness.

As I wish myself to be safe from harm, so I wish you to be safe.
May you be happy and peaceful.
May you be strong and healthy.
May you take care of yourself with joy.

(Continue for some time.)

Expand the loving-kindness outside the building. Imagine the people walking by, the birds and squirrels and other animals. Include people driving by or flying overhead.

I wish you well.
May you be happy . . .

(Continue for some time.)

Feel the loving-kindness grow so much that you can include all the people in the world, no matter what their color or faith.

May you be happy . . .

(Continue for some time.)

The metta is so strong that you can share it with difficult people as well.

For all the harm you have done, I forgive you.
May you be happy . . .

(Continue for some time.)

Feel the loving-kindness overflow so that you can include every creature who has ever been born and every creature who will be born in the future.

May we be safe from harm.
May we be happy and peaceful.
May we be strong and healthy.
May we take care of ourselves with joy.

Your heart has opened so much that it can hold every being with care and affection.

Rest in the feeling of loving-kindness for all beings.
(Silently rest in metta.)

Practicing metta is like planting a seed. Over time loving-kindness blossoms to include everyone. We begin to realize that all beings deserve unconditional love, including ourselves. Eventually we find that we are relating to others with kindness, generosity, and acceptance. That's the gift of metta.

Six

Embracing Difficulties

KARUNA AND TONGLEN PRACTICES

One day I visit eighty-six-year-old Katherine who can barely speak and is paler than the sheets on her bed. I have determined that this is the day I will pray for someone and that is foremost in my mind. As I introduce myself to her, she struggles to say something. I lean closer in an effort to decipher her words by listening carefully and reading her lips. After many tries I get the sound "puh." This is my opportunity!

"Would you like a prayer?" I ask solicitously.

She struggles further, "puh ee." I don't understand.

"Puh ee eez."

"Please," I repeat.

"Wuh!" she says again and again, and with difficulty raises her hand to her mouth.

"Water! You want some water!"

She closes her eyes in relief. I look around the room for a cup with a straw and some water and find none. I go to the nurses' station and am told that she cannot have water. When I return to her room all I'm allowed to do is moisten her lips with a lollipop-like sponge. She grabs it in her mouth and sucks greedily. I want so much to be able to give her what she wants, just as I want to end all my patients' suffering.

I am reminded of the poem of Ryokan, the eighteenth-century Zen hermit monk:

O, that my priest's robe were wide enough
to gather up all the suffering people
In this floating world.

At the beginning of my chaplaincy training, I interpreted the poem to mean that I could change things, fix things. I believed that if I were compassionate and wise enough I could end suffering, just as when I was a child my mother kissed my scraped knee to make the hurt go away.

Now I see that the poem means to be present to all the world's pain, to bear witness and honor it, to take it in as my own. So there is no distinction between the caregiver and the patient. No separation.

My peer group has been after me to begin to say prayers with patients, but I find it very difficult. How can I pray to a God I don't believe in? How can I say the words with conviction—won't the patients see through the charade? What it really comes down to is my lack of "pastoral identity"—I don't fully see myself as a spiritual presence.

My solution is to search through old Christian and Jewish prayer books, spiritual poetry and journals, culling those fragments of prayers that I can say from my heart and that I think will be meaningful to patients. I carefully design and typeset them on my computer and place the pages in a small ring binder. I make a cover from a snippet of tapestry and carry the book with me on my rounds—a talisman. It is my anchor; if I'm in a situation where I feel at a loss I can always refer to it.

Although I rarely use the book, it was important for me to make the effort, to try to grasp the similarities between my Buddhist beliefs and those of other faiths, rather than dwell on the differences. The day I visit Katherine, after allowing her to suck as much water as I dare, these words spontaneously pour out:

May you be free from pain.
May you be free from suffering.
May your heart be filled with peace.

Placing my hand on Katherine's head, I say these words from my heart and mean them. I feel an authentic desire for her to be free from pain and suffering, just as I wish myself to be free from pain and suffering. I wish both of us to experience peace and serenity and acceptance. These words are my prayer.

During my first year of working in the hospital with dying patients I couldn't sleep, had psychosomatic leg pains, and grew inordinately attached to patients who died. The loss and grief were overwhelming. They would flow into me, get trapped, and build up until bursting forth at inopportune times as tears. I fooled myself by saying this meant I was truly a caring person. The truth was, I didn't know how to react to suffering because I had erected a barrier around myself that kept me insulated from my own pain.

In order to break the wall of denial of my own suffering, I had to immerse myself in the suffering of others. Only then would I be able to confront my own.

Many of the professional caregivers that I work with have the same dilemma—they are overwhelmed with pity and so leave their professions, or they become cold and uncaring in the face of suffering.

■

KARUNA

You will recall that metta is the first of the brahma viharas or divine abodes. The second is compassion, *karuna*. The feeling of compassion is likened to a pleasant quivering of the heart in response to pain.

How difficult it was for me to understand that it's not necessary to break into tears and rend my garments in order to express caring. Karuna practice helps us to feel compassion for others without being overwhelmed by grief. We begin to understand that pity is not compassion, and that it is not necessary to be cruel in order to protect ourselves from pain.

There is a place where there is no separation between the one suffering and the caregiver. There is just pain, which can be taken in and let go.

When practicing karuna, we generally start with another person. Pick someone who is ill, but not too ill. Or choose someone who is undergoing mental suffering. It's important to kindle the spark of compassion and, as with metta, it's the feeling that's important, not the words.

The phrases that I usually work with are:

May you be free from pain.
May you be free from suffering.
May your heart be filled with peace.

Guided Meditation

Sit in a position that you can hold comfortably for several minutes, and close your eyes.

First take a couple of really deep breaths, being aware of your breath going in and out, feeling your chest rising and falling.

Take an image of someone who is suffering, place it in your heart, and surround it with tenderness and care.

Repeat silently to yourself:

May you be free from pain.
May you be free from suffering.
May your heart be filled with peace.

Each time you say the phrases have a strong sense or image of the person to whom you are sending karuna.

> May you be free from pain.
> May you be free from suffering.
> May your heart be filled with peace.

If it is helpful, imagine the heart so filled with peace that it overflows, sending the well-being to others who are suffering.

Keep repeating the phrases until you feel a gentle tugging of the heart in response to the person's pain, then let the phrases go and rest in compassion. When your mind wanders, come back to the sensation of your breath going in and out, your chest rising and falling, and the phrases.

(Meditate on your own for several minutes.)

If you would like to, send the compassion to yourself.

> May I be free from pain.
> May I be free from suffering.
> May my heart be filled with peace.

When you're ready, open your eyes and come back to the room.

Were you able to feel the "pleasant quiver of the heart in response to pain"? If so, did you notice any change in the quality of the feeling when you shifted to yourself as the one receiving karuna?

All of the brahma vihara practices are meant to change our own relationship to difficult situations and emotions. In the case of karuna, we're dealing with the suffering that results from our relationship to physical, emotional, and spiritual pain. Pain is a given, suffering is extra.

Pain and Suffering

If you burn your hand, it's going to hurt. If you've practiced mindfulness meditation, you've learned to follow your breath and to identify the pain as "sensation." As you become aware of the nuances of the sensation, you'll be able to label it "unpleasant."

You can explore further by noticing the feelings and thoughts that arise as a result of the unpleasant sensation: annoyance, aversion, frustration, anger, self-pity, fear. Then the attention switches to the quality of mental suffering. As you connect yourself more firmly with what's occurring in the present moment, you realize that the quality of the pain changes and you are not trapped by it. The pain becomes manageable.

Karuna helps us address the mental suffering that arises when we see pain in others or ourselves. It creates a fluid space where we bear witness to the suffering.

Going Deeper

I don't understand why we have to practice compassion; doesn't it arise naturally?

It can, but often it is tinged with desire and aversion—wanting to relieve pain or denying that pain exists. By practicing karuna, we are training ourselves to clearly see what exists, without desire or aversion. We remove the dark glasses of pity or cruelty. Only then can we act with wisdom.

For example, in Katherine's case, my entire being cried out to give her as much water as she wanted, but that would have been detrimental to her health. I would have been acting on my own desires—to be the one who grants her wishes, to be seen as a good person, and perhaps to quench the desire in her eyes, so that *I* would not suffer. Karuna practice helps us to find a balance between pity and cruelty.

I've been a hospice nurse for several years. At first I would get close to my patients and their families. All the patients died, and I couldn't bear the sense of loss anymore. Now I do my job, but never get involved with my charges. I don't feel anything and am thinking of quitting.

You may have avoided the pain, but suffering is still there. It seems that you've gone from one end of the spectrum to the other and both are uncomfortable. To come back to the center, use the phrase: "I care about your pain." During meditation call up the image of a patient and for a couple of minutes repeat the phrase, "I care about your pain." Then move on to the next patient, and the next.

If you don't have a regular meditation practice, then take one or two deep breaths before you enter your patient's room and silently say to yourself, "(patient's name) I care about your pain." You will notice that the quality of the attention that you bring to the visit has altered. The inner tension that constricts your feelings will ease. Patients will sense your softening and you'll be able to work with them in a more comfortable way.

You may feel that this is dishonest, but simply saying the words, "I care about your pain," implies a willingness to care. In some self-help programs this approach is called "acting as if." Just forming a conscious intention to care is the beginning of the softening process.

Karuna practice changes *our own* relationship with pain and helps us to act from a centered place.

And remember to have compassion for your own suffering. Few people can work with the dying forever. Take a sabbatical and treat yourself to a long vacation or retreat. Then, if you decide to change professions, it's okay. You may be ready to move on to your next challenge.

Because of chemotherapy for breast cancer I've lost my hair, have no energy, and feel dreadful. Can I do compassion practice for myself?
Yes, but be careful, because underlying anger or self-pity might come to the surface. "Oh, I'll never be free from suffering" spirals downward to "No one else has side effects this bad" and plummets to "Why me?" Karuna is a purification practice, so it's natural that these thoughts will arise even if they've been deeply buried. If you feel ready to deal with them, then do so.

However, it might be more skillful to use the metta phrases for yourself: "May I be safe from harm, May I be happy and peaceful, May I be strong and healthy, May I take care of myself with joy." You could replace one of them with, "May my heart be filled with peace."

When we're experiencing a difficult time, we sometimes forget that others are suffering just as we are. One of my Zen teachers battled cancer for several years. She received many letters from others who were undergoing cancer treatment. When they asked what they could do, she replied, "Find someone worse off than you are and help her."

This is the spirit of compassion. The driving force is not to ignore our own pain, but to connect to others who are experiencing pain so that we understand that each of us experiences pain in life. The mental agony that entangles us when we become ill or our partner dies arises just like thoughts and memories do during meditation. Self-pity, fear, anxiety, rage are the hindrances magnified a thousand times. Can you sit quietly with these emotions and note, "Oh, self-pity is arising"? Can you begin to know that each of us has pain in our lives? No one escapes.

A long, long time ago, during the Buddha's lifetime, a woman was beside herself with grief because her newborn child had died. She carried the body around hoping that someone could bring him back to life. Finally, she approached the Buddha.

"Please return my child to me. Please bring him back to life."

The Buddha said, "Bring me a mustard seed from a house that has not experienced death, and I will help you."

The woman went to every hut in the village, but could find no household that had not experienced the death of a parent or child or sister or brother.

Desolate, she returned to the Buddha.

"I have not been able to find a single person who has not experienced a death."

The Buddha looked into her eyes and stroked her head, "Everyone must experience sickness, old age, and death."

The woman bowed her head in understanding and left to bury her child.

Try sending karuna to other persons who have cancer, particularly those who are in the same support group. When the feeling of compassion is steady, imagine yourself in the group and adjust the phrases to "May *we* be free from pain," and so on.

When I try to do this meditation for my dying father, I get so angry that he's ill that I can't continue.

When a strong emotion arises, it is hard to concentrate on the phrases. Return to the mindfulness practice for a time. Drop the story of why you're angry. Stay with the physical sensations, paying close attention to where the anger rests in the body—its size, texture, temperature. When you feel able to coexist with the sensations, then return to the phrases. If you're not able to do this at this time, be kind and send metta to yourself.

Making the Practice Your Own

⬧ Try to uncover the difference between compassion and pity. On a sheet of paper make two columns, one headed "Compassion is . . . " and the other, "Pity is . . . ." In each column write adjectives and nouns that you associate with the word. Then write a long sentence using those words. Can you write a story using those words?

⬧ If you are a visual person, try making abstract representations of compassion and pity, focusing on the differences.

⬧ Repeat the above exercises with the word *cruelty.*

⬧ When you visit a friend or family member who's very ill, stop before you enter his room. Take a couple of deep breaths, being aware of your breath going in and out, feeling your chest rising and falling, and silently say to yourself, "(name), I care about your pain." When you go in, take a seat next to the bed. When you ask how he is doing—wait for the answer and listen with your full attention. Silence is okay; it's not necessary to make small talk. If you feel awkward, follow your breath and silently repeat the karuna phrase, "May you be free from pain," or simply, "I care about your pain."

- Every evening on the news we learn about another war, disaster, or atrocity. It's impossible to travel to each place as a volunteer or even to send money to every cause. That doesn't mean that you cannot connect with the suffering. Whenever you become aware of a disaster, silently say the karuna phrases:

> May you be free from pain.
> May you be free from suffering.
> May your heart be filled with peace.
>> or
> I care about your pain.

- Try walking meditation while saying the karuna phrases or using a mala.

Mudita

The companion practice of karuna, or compassion, is *mudita*, or sympathetic joy. Karuna is a pleasant tugging of the heart in response to suffering; mudita is joy at the good fortune of others. For some of us karuna is easy, while mudita is difficult. I think it has to do with our own self-esteem or lack of it.

When we encounter someone who is suffering, we might experience a subtle separation, a sense that we are better than the person who's suffering. When someone gets a job that we want or buys a luxury car, we may feel that we are shortchanged. In both cases we feel separate.

Mudita is a practice that opens our hearts further by helping us to know that there is enough for everyone. It is the antidote to jealousy and envy.

Work with the phrase, "May your happiness and success never end," or "I wish you joy."

Going Deeper

I can't imagine ever being happy at the success of another.

When we begin to practice the brahma viharas, divine abodes, in depth, there is a sequence. First we work with loving-kindness until we can generate the feeling for ourselves. Until we come to love and accept ourselves exactly as we are, we will have difficulty caring about the joys and sorrows of others. But even if you have no opportunity to practice the divine abodes over a long period, you can still reap the benefits when you form the intention to experience mudita.

My own state of serenity and loving-kindness can always be gauged by how envious or jealous I am. Sometimes everything is fine; other times when I read about someone who has attained a success that I crave, I experience a stabbing in my gut. I've learned to stay with the physical sensation, noticing its nuances. Then I gently note, "Oh, I'm jealous again." Finally, I am able to say to the lucky person, "I wish you well." Now my fits of envy don't arise so often, and when they do, they are not overwhelming storms, but brief showers.

Mindfulness plus mudita allows us to become aware of, accept, and transform our difficulties.

Upekkha

The jewel in the crown of the brahma viharas is *upekkha* (equanimity). When we attain upekkha we no longer view life as a roller coaster taking us from exciting highs to devastating lows. We are able to keep our balance no matter what comes up.

When the last winter Olympic Games were televised, I noticed a skiing event called moguls. The side of the mountain was sculpted into bumps of different heights, positioned in no particular order. In between were deep, narrow valleys. The skiers had to descend the mountain as quickly as possible while navigating the moguls. Those who were fastest touched neither the tops of the moguls, nor the valleys. They maintained a steady course, just grazing the bumps at mid-height.

That's what equanimity is like. When sickness, old age, and death occur, we hold a steady course. When we win the lottery or a race or fall in love, we maintain our balance.

The traditional phrases for equanimity practice are:

> All beings are the authors of their own karma.
>   or
> Things are as they are.

When you begin to feel overwhelmed by feelings of powerlessness, it is helpful to use one of these phrases.

One day at a Zen center, a woman came running up to me, shouting, "You didn't consult me and you hurt my feelings! You're such a bully! You're a terrible person!" I admit I felt shaken—am I a terrible person?

Later on during the same day, a young man thanked me for helping him with a problem. "You are so kind and compassionate, I hope to be like you someday." I would have been gratified, but I burst into laughter. Things are as they are.

The truth is that I'm terrible, but I'm also compassionate. Praise and blame do not last. Can I avoid aversion to blame and attachment to praise? Equanimity clears the mind of hindrances so that we can act appropriately. Perhaps I can soften some of my bullying qualities.

Going Deeper

Do you mean that if people get sick they brought it on themselves?

In some branches of Buddhism one of the prime tenets is the law of karma—because of *this, that* occurs, or more colloquially, what goes around, comes around. They believe each of us lives many lifetimes, during which our karma is resolved and we are purified.

For some people belief in karma nurtures hope and acceptance in the midst of difficulties, because they believe they are atoning for evil actions committed during past lives and preparing themselves to attain nirvana. Others find appalling the concept that contracting AIDS or cancer or ALS is our own fault. This idea ties into the Western belief in a punishing god: Why did this happen to me? What did I do wrong? How can I make it go away? When I work with patients who come from that kind of faith tradition, I use the phrase, "Things are as they are."

Equanimity doesn't worry about the how's or why's. It simply rests in the present moment, being present with what is. Things are as they are.

Equanimity sounds dull. I look forward to the excitement that comes when something wonderful happens. Why would I want to give it up?

How about giving up suffering? Equanimity is the middle road between attachment and aversion. You may desire the good times and then want to hold on to them; eventually fear that they will end robs you of your enjoyment. When something terrible occurs, chances are you don't look forward to that kind of excitement. You want to push it away.

Equanimity practice brings us back to the present moment. Our hearts begin to expand to take in the good times as well as the bad. We know that nothing lasts forever and that everything changes.

True joy comes from within; it does not depend on outer circumstances. Once discovered it is always with us.

Equanimity seems cold and uncaring.

The near enemy of equanimity is indifference. They look alike, but indifference is selfish. We are so involved in our own lives and stories that we can't be bothered with anything that does not directly affect our own search for happiness and avoidance of pain. An earthquake in Central America, a drought in Africa, a train crash in Asia, a war in Europe? So what! Unless travel plans are affected or relatives live there, we turn the dial on the TV and tune out.

True equanimity is based on wisdom and compassion. Because we *know* that all things are impermanent, that everything is in the long run unsatisfactory, and that there is no separate self, we simply act appropriately.

Here's a Zen story:

A long, long time ago, a hermit monk lived in a hut on the outskirts of a village. A young girl became pregnant and accused the monk of being the father. The angry villagers surrounded his hut, berating him for breaking his vows and harming the girl.

The monk said, "Is that so?"

When the baby was born, the girl's parents didn't want to raise the child. They brought the baby to the monk and said, "Since you fathered this child, it's your responsibility to take care of it!"

The monk said, "Is that so?"

He raised the child for several years, lovingly feeding it and making sure it was always warm and clean.

The girl began to feel remorse for having given up her child. She went to her parents and revealed the name of the boy who was the real father of her child. Together the family went to the monk, apologized for lying about him, and claimed their child.

The monk said, "Is that so?" and returned the child to its mother.

The monk did not make excuses or try to defend himself. He simply did what needed to be done without attachment or aversion.

We practice metta, which is unconditional love directed to all beings. We then work with connecting with people's sorrows (karuna) and their joys (mudita). Only then can we find the middle ground of upekkha, equanimity. It's raining? Open an umbrella. A homeless person is hungry? Give him a sandwich. Your house is on fire? Call the fire department. No moaning and groaning—just do it. That's equanimity.

Equanimity sounds passive. With such horrible things going on in the world, I think we should demonstrate, raise money, do whatever it takes to try to make things better.

Twelve-step programs have embraced this Serenity Prayer:

God grant me the serenity
to accept the things I cannot change,
the courage to change the things I can,
and the wisdom to know the difference.

Only when we are serene, when we have found the middle ground between greed and anger, will we be able to act appropriately. There's nothing wrong with protesting against nuclear power plants or discrimination or a war. It's *how* we do it. Can we put aside blame and anger and violence to act from a place of love? Gandhi did; so did Martin Luther King, Jr. Can you?

TONGLEN

Tonglen is a Tibetan Buddhist practice that I find akin to the brahma vihara practices that help us to relate to things as they are. We practice the brahma viharas by starting with ourselves and gradually moving on to benefactors, friends, neutral persons, and difficult people. Eventually we can open to everyone's pain with loving-kindness and compassion, no matter who they are.

In tonglen we also can start with ourselves, then move on to take on the suffering of dear friends, neutral people, difficult persons, and all beings. But tonglen is tougher than karuna. Karuna is gentle, acknowledging that there is difficulty, helping us accept and befriend the difficulty. Tonglen asks us to viscerally take in difficult emotions such as fear and anger, as well as physical pain and suffering. Instead of pushing away the pain, we take it in, experiencing it fully. Then we transform it into compassion and loving-kindness.

Barbara has a strong spiritual connection that has supported her during her work with people living with AIDS. Several years ago, Barbara's son committed suicide and this has been the underlying motif of her life.

As she was driving to a day's retreat for professional care-givers, anger about her son's death erupted again. During the retreat she practiced the various meditations that were offered, but tonglen was the one that helped her.

She imagined all the mothers and fathers who were in her situation and breathed in all their common anger and suffering. Then she sent out the cool, light, and bright breath to them. After the meditation she told the group that she felt cleansed and in some way hopeful.

Tonglen was the only thing that worked for her. Barbara no longer felt isolated; she connected with all the parents who had lost children to suicide, and she felt as if she were easing their pain as well as her own. There seemed to be a light at the end of the tunnel of her grief.

To begin to practice tonglen, choose an emotion that is caus-ing you distress, but not too much distress—it's important to build up the tonglen muscles. When we are comfortable with the practice we can move on to more challenging emotions or situations.

Guided Meditation

For several minutes breathe in and out mindfully, until you're resting in a quiet space.

Choose an emotion that is causing difficulty in your life.

When you're ready, envision the difficult emotion as smoke. It is heavy, dark, and hot.

Breathe in the heavy, dark, hot smoke through your nose.

Take it in as fully as you can, feeling it go down your throat into your chest and abdomen.

Feel the smoke transform into light, bright, and cool as you exhale through your mouth.

Take in the emotion with your whole body and send out the brightness through every pore of your skin.

Know throughout that the smoke *is* your difficult emotion and is being transformed.

(Continue to practice for some time, breathing in heavy, dark, hot—breathing out light, bright, and cool.)

After some time imagine all the other people experiencing the same emotion.

Breathe in their distress as well as your own, and when you send out the healing energy of light, bright, and cool, send it to everyone who is experiencing that difficult emotion.

(Continue to practice silently.)

May all beings be filled with light and joy.

In tonglen we inhale through the nose and exhale through the mouth. You may notice that because of the emphasis on visualization your breath feels more controlled and becomes deeper and slower. This is okay and may help center you. Try not to force the breath. Imagine the smoke entering your nostrils like an aroma and follow its path to the abdomen. As you release the breath, notice how the aroma becomes fresh and clean as it rises up and out through your mouth.

Try tonglen for others who are suffering. For this meditation, start with someone close to you who is ill.

Guided Meditation

First take a couple of deep breaths, being aware of your breath going in and out, feeling your chest rising and falling.

Continue to follow your breath mindfully, until you reach a quiet, clear space.

Now visualize a dear friend who's ill.

As you breathe in, imagine taking in all his pain and suffering, all his fear and sadness.

When you breathe out, send out healing, love, and joy.

Breathe in pain.

Breathe out healing.

Breathe in fear.

Breathe out love.

Breathe in sadness.

Breathe out joy.

Continue to take in your friend's suffering for a time. (Silent meditation.)

When you are ready, imagine all the other people who share your friend's illness.

Feel your heart expand to take in their suffering as well.

Breathe in pain and suffering, fear and sadness.

Breathe out healing, love, and joy.

Breathe in pain.

Breathe out healing.

Breathe in fear.

Breathe out love.

Breathe in sadness.

Breathe out joy.

(Continue for some time in silent meditation.)

May all beings be healed in mind, body, and spirit.

Jane is a cancer survivor who is quite restless and has difficulty meditating. During a retreat where we practiced several kinds of meditation, she was able to breathe in the cancer of all the friends in her support group and send out healing to them. Tonglen empowered her.

At the same retreat a nurse had difficulty with all of the meditations except tonglen. She also felt empowered by it as she worked with the lingering resentment from a divorce.

Be brave. Be willing not only to face your suffering, but also to take it inside yourself, to become your suffering. Then you can transform it and include others in the healing.

Going Deeper

This seems like an upside-down meditation. I was taught to breathe in the light and breathe out the bad stuff.

One of the reasons I haven't used tonglen much is that some people have learned to breathe in the light and breathe out the dark. It is confusing when I tell them to do the opposite.

I find breathing out the bad stuff to be subtly damaging. It trains us in attachment and aversion. We want everything to be pleasant, and when any disruption occurs our first impulse is to push it away.

In all the Buddhist meditations in this book the key is to become aware of, accept, and befriend *everything* in our lives. Tonglen accomplishes this in an assertive way. It is a warrior's practice. We form the intention not only to come face-to-face with our difficulties, but to absorb them, to allow them to enter our body and become a part of us. Then we let them go.

When I visualize the smoke coming in my nose I feel my throat tighten and I'm afraid I'll choke.

This is one of the reasons that tonglen is a difficult practice. Our resistance to dealing with painful emotions is deeply ingrained. There is no need for you to practice tonglen at this time. Just say to yourself, "Not yet," and return to metta or karuna.

However, it may be that the image of smoke is causing you distress. Try again, thinking of a gray cloud that is dark and heavy, and as you exhale imagine that it's dissipating, revealing the clear bright sky.

I had an interesting experience when I was doing tonglen. As the meditation progressed, the smoke itself became less dense. I really felt that the emotion I was working with lightened as well.

Tonglen works. But be careful not to expect this to happen each time you practice tonglen. Remember that everything changes. You may not have the same experience each time you meditate, but that does not mean it's not working.

If I try to take in all the suffering of others—for example my friends who have cancer—can I get sick, too?

You won't contract cancer, but the meditation is quite powerful. You may actually feel some pain. I suggest that you not do this meditation unless you are in a very deep, relaxed state. Keep the tonglen brief and end with a calming mindfulness or loving-kindness meditation for yourself.

Vera has lived with leukemia for twenty-four years. She almost died during the first year, but then the disease vanished. She attributes this to her great faith in Jesus and to the healing powers of her Peruvian grandma, who is a shaman. Vera has inherited some of her grandma's powers, and during the past ten years she has occasionally healed others.

She told me that sometimes the connection with her subjects is so strong that the pain leaves their body and enters hers. Vera has learned to husband her own strength and she works with others only when a case particularly touches her and she feels strong.

If tonglen frightens you, then you're not ready to do it. Perhaps you could look at your fear mindfully as we learned in Chapter Three. If you want to include others in your meditation, try metta or karuna.

I can't do this practice at all; it's terrifying.
You don't have to, and you don't have to feel bad about it. Over the years I've been drawn to different kinds of meditation at different times. Sometimes it depends on what's going on in my life; sometimes it may be the phases of the moon. Remember that meditation is to help you, not to make your life more complicated. Stick with what works for you.

I was leery of using tonglen in my work with people who are very ill because it seemed harsh. The truth, which I discovered much later, is that I was projecting my own fear on them.

Each of us is unique; some people respond to metta, others prefer tonglen. I have found that people who've been meditating for a long time are able to practice tonglen, as are people who have reached the end of their rope.

I remember a dying AIDS patient who was filled with rage at the disease and at his family who had abandoned him. He himself had helped many friends as they died. No one was left to care for him. Tonglen opened his heart. Taking in the suffering of all those who were suffering as he was and including them in the healing out-breath connected him to others. He no longer felt alone.

During a workshop at a county jail, I asked the inmates to notice where in their bodies their rage or frustration or stress manifested. After following the breath and noticing the sensation, we began tonglen. One young man told me that as the meditation progressed, the knot in his chest that held his anger loosened and he felt relief. Sometimes it's more terrifying not to practice tonglen.

Making the Practice Your Own

❖ Try tonglen as a forgiveness practice. Call to mind a time when you acted in a way that was harmful to others. When you breathe in, take in the full responsibility for your actions. As you exhale, send out understanding and healing. After doing this meditation, do you feel your heart opening? Does the desire to seek forgiveness from the other person arise? Can you find the courage to seek reconciliation?

❖ When you are touched by some tragedy, practice tonglen to relieve the suffering of others. Take in the suffering of all the victims, making it your own, and send out the cool, light, bright healing.

❖ Practice the tonglen visualization for sick or dying friends.

Relieving the Suffering of Others

Lately there has been interest in the power of intercessory prayer in healing, generated by new books and research. Tonglen, along with karuna and the other brahma viharas, feels most like prayer. Although we are not asking a deity to remove suffering, all of our energy and attention are focused on relieving another's suffering. The intention to heal is present.

Changing our own relationship to pain and suffering is the purpose of some of the brahma viharas and tonglen. They are spiritually and emotionally healing. But if personal prayer is not part of your tradition, these meditations can be used to wish others well.

Most of us feel uncomfortable when we have to visit someone who's very ill or dying. We don't know what to do or say. Because we are afraid of saying the wrong thing, we say nothing at all. We miss true intimacy because of our own fear of sickness, old age, and death.

Karuna and tonglen can open our hearts so that we can be with our friends and family members during their deaths.

A few days before Christmas, Glenda is drifting in and out of coma. Her estranged daughters are unsure of themselves and awkward in the face of death. They wish to communicate with their mother, but feel she cannot hear them. I assure them that hearing is the last sense to go and that Glenda will feel their presence. Still they have no words.

"Do you sing?" I ask.

One sister giggles, but they agree to sing to Glenda. As I leave the room, they confer as to what to sing and make an awkward start on "Jingle Bells."

A couple of hours later, my beeper goes off and I'm told that Glenda is dead. When I return to her room, the oldest sister tells me that their mother died while they were singing:

Silent night, holy night,
All is calm, all is bright,
'Round yon virgin, Mother and Child,
Holy infant, so tender and mild.
Sleep in heavenly peace,
Sleep in heavenly peace.

Although the women did not pray in the literal sense, they formed a prayerful intention. Glenda had been holding on to life with her fingernails, and the joyful chorus of her daughters' voices helped her to let go. Not all healing is physical. The communion between the daughters healed a long-time rift as they surrounded Glenda with harmony, the music's as well as their own.

Making the Practice Your Own

We can connect to others' suffering in different ways.

- ❖ Find out your friend's favorite poet and read poetry aloud to him.

- ❖ Bring her music and listen to it with her.

- ❖ Share his interests: playing chess, doing crossword puzzles, watching a video tape.

- ❖ Make a photo album for her.

- ❖ Bring his favorite food or drink.

- ❖ Ask about a memorable incident from her youth. Listen when she tells you.

- ❖ Sing together.

- ❖ Laugh together.

- ❖ Pray together.

- ❖ Meditate together.

Karuna and tonglen meditation practices help change our relationship to difficulties. When we are able to straddle the middle ground between pity and coldness, we can trust ourselves to act from a centered place. We can act appropriately, doing what needs to be done.

Seven

Letting Go

It's easy to die.
Just give your breath
back to the trees
and wind.

PETER LEVITT, *ONE HUNDRED BUTTERFLIES*

CO-MEDITATION

Martha has been filled with resentment lately. Even though she is undergoing chemotherapy for cancer, her sisters are not willing to help care for their father, who is dying. Little by little, Martha's privacy has been eaten away and her husband's and children's lives disrupted. Her father uses the downstairs guest bedroom, and the bathroom is for his use only; her mother sleeps in the study. The living room is filled with a commode, urinal, and boxes of medical paraphernalia. Martha's house has been turned over to her father, and she has little time or space to nurture herself and her children.

Usually I visit her at her home and we practice loving-kindness meditation, but on this day, Martha is able to find someone to stay with her father and so she has come to Peaceful Dwelling.

We enter the sunlit meditation room, and when she reclines on the cushions, I place a pillow under her head, cover her body with a blanket, and begin to practice co-meditation.

After the meditation (about twenty minutes), Martha seems to be sleeping. I quietly leave the zendo and allow her to rest. When she awakens an hour later, she tells me this is the first nap she's had in weeks. She has been able to let go of her resentment for a brief time.

In previous chapters we've explored ways of facing our emotions and befriending them. But sometimes it's impossible for a person in great distress to practice in this way. She may need help to be able to let go of anger, fear, and even life. Having a person sharing your breath helps to let go.

In the Tibetan tradition of Buddhism, great emphasis is placed on achieving a peaceful death. The moment of death is considered the optimum time to attain nirvana, thus ending the cycle of rebirth. There are many visualizations and meditations to achieve this serenity, both at the moment of death and after death. Although co-meditation, meditating with and for another, was originally used with the dying to ease the transition between life and death, it can be used in any situation where a strong emotion causes havoc with the mind and body.

Guided Meditation

Find a partner to practice with. The patient will lie on a bed or the floor, while the caregiver sits or kneels next to him. The caregiver will do the guiding as the patient closes his eyes and lies still in a comfortable position with toes slightly pointed out. The caregiver begins the guided relaxation and pauses as long as seems necessary between the phrases.

Bring your attention to the tips of your toes and imagine that they are relaxing.

Feel the relaxation moving up your calves, into your knees.

Your thighs are beginning to relax. Feel the relaxation move into your hips.

Notice how the lower part of your body feels light and easy.

Let the ease move into your abdomen, heart, and chest.

Feel the relaxation move up your neck.

Your chin is relaxing. Your mouth is relaxing. Your nose and eyes are relaxing.

The space between your eyes is relaxing.

Imagine the relaxation moving over the top of your head, down the back of your head, down your neck.

Feel your shoulders relax, and be aware of the relaxation moving down your arms into your hands and fingers.

Imagine any tightness or tension in your body leaving through the tips of your toes and fingers.

Take a moment to enjoy the feeling of all the muscles of your body working together in harmony with no tightness, no tension.

I am now going to make the universal sound of letting go. As you exhale, I will say "ah."

Would you like to say this with me? (If yes, have the patient aspirate "ah" only four or five times, then ask him to remain silent, listening to the sound of your voice.)

Each time you exhale imagine all your anger (or fear or sadness) leaving your body.

"Ah!" What a relief it is to let the anger go.

(Carefully watch the chest or abdomen, wherever the breath is more apparent, rise with each in-breath. As the patient exhales, say "ah," drawing the sound out to match the length of the breath. Continue for some time, whatever is comfortable for you or the patient.)

Notice how light your body feels.

Notice the well-being that has replaced the anger.

When you open your eyes, the pleasant sensation of letting go will remain with you throughout the day, and whenever the anger arises again, take a couple of really deep breaths and say "ah," releasing all negativity.

When I demonstrate this meditation at workshops, the volunteer "patients" are deeply moved. One nurse said she could feel my hands move over her body, and as I mentioned different parts of her body they became warm. (Even when the onlookers told her I hadn't moved my hands, she remained skeptical.) Another time an older man began to cry and later in a private talk said that some major knot in his psyche had loosened. In all cases, the patient felt a deep sense of connection with me.

Some workshop participants think that the strong feelings are a product of my years of meditation practice, but when I have them pair off to practice, they experience the same sense of connection and release.

When we share the breath of life with others, we become a part of them. They are not alone and we are not alone. We become what is known in the Zen tradition, as "not one, not two."

Going Deeper

I experienced a deep connection with my partner and was brought to tears.

How often do we really pay attention to others? While they are talking, we barely listen because we are so busy planning what we want to say. Rarely does conversation occur. Usually we engage in two monologues bumping into one another. When we practice co-meditation with another, we watch the in-breath and out-breath with full attention as if our own lives depended on it. We are connected in a special way.

The tears may arise from a place of deep connection. We remember what it was like to be one with everything. The breath is intimate. We are born with each in-breath and we die with each out-breath. By breathing with another we become their life and death.

In the exercise I was the patient. I imagined I was dying, and when my partner breathed with me, I no longer felt alone.

We are never alone, but we don't realize it. The silence helps to connect you with your partner. A sense of intimacy and caring grows without words. It's the intention that matters. Your partner put aside his own agenda in order to be fully present with you. In his presence all the universe was included.

How can we do this meditation with a deaf person?

One of the participants at a weekend workshop was deaf. She could get along well in her daily life because she read lips. However, watching my lips took too much effort and she was not able to relax. While she watched me I explained what we were going to do, and I asked her to imagine her body relaxing and to form the intention of letting go. We experimented, and although I continued to aspirate the "ah" sound, I stroked her hand as I exhaled. She reported that this worked for her. We tend to think that words are our only means of communication, but touch is a more intimate way of interacting.

The person I was working with was restless and his breath was erratic.

You may need skillful means to bring the person to a relaxed state. After the guided relaxation, instead of going directly to the "ah" sound, ask him to count the exhalations with you. Count from one to ten. If the breath still hasn't evened out, begin again. This time only you will say the numbers aloud. Ask him to visualize each number as you say it and to hold the image until the sound stops. Continue in this manner until you feel comfortable switching to the "ah" sound.

I'd like to do this with my sister who's dying from cancer, but she seems reluctant.

Perhaps she's not ready to let go of life. No matter how much we wish to help others have a peaceful death, it's really up to them. Perhaps she would be willing to practice letting go of nagging resentment or fear instead. Try using the word *releasing* instead of *letting go*. If this is not successful, meditate for her privately.

I felt drained when I finished the meditation even though it was only ten minutes long.

You use an enormous amount of energy to stay concentrated on the person's breath. One way to conserve strength is to gradually lower your voice until the "ah" becomes merely a deep sigh.

A benefit for your own practice is that your focus is being strengthened. Initially, do the meditation for a brief period, then work up to longer periods.

When someone is dying it may be helpful to form a co-meditation chain. Gather a group of friends and family members and take turns being the caregiver. When one person gets tired, another can take over. This serves a dual purpose. Sometimes those surrounding a dying person feel at a loss because it seems they can do nothing. Co-meditation is a practice that an extended family can do. They feel part of the process, and the dying person senses their caring presence.

At the end of the meditation, you say to carry the feeling of letting go into the day. How about the person who's on her deathbed?

When you are finished breathing with the person, you can move onto the *phowa* meditation for the dying (see page 120)

My aunt is very religious. How can I make this meditation meaningful to her?

After you've practiced the "ah" sound for some time, you can switch to a brief phrase that is important to her, for example, "Christ have mercy." If you look at this practice closely, you can see that it is a concentration practice that matches the breath to a mantra.

How can I use this with someone in coma?

You can skip the relaxation phase of the meditation. Simply introduce yourself to the patient (even if he seems comatose) and tell him that you're going to sit with him for a while. Touch his hand and begin to silently breathe with him. Exhale through your mouth. The breath is then more audible than normal, and it's not necessary to say "ah."

One day I visited an old woman in intensive care. The nurse on duty told me that the woman was near death and that her family was in the waiting room. It was my job to break the news to them. When I suggested that they might want to say good-bye to her, they refused. This was beyond my comprehension.

Again I asked, "Wouldn't you like to sit with her for a while?" The answer was a resounding no.

I returned to the ICU and sat beside the woman, breathing with her. After some time, a nurse checked the monitors—her breath had slowed, along with her heartbeat. She seemed to be in less distress, and I sat with her until her last breath.

It is such a privilege to be present at the end of a person's life. Unfortunately, our own fear of death inhibits us and we miss this intimate moment. Practicing co-meditation can take us out of our own fear. By concentrating on another's breath, we are practicing living in the present moment. When we learn to live in the present, we will be able to be present for death—our own or another's.

Is this meditation only for a person who is dying?

As I mentioned earlier, I use co-meditation to help people work with difficult emotions. Some psychotherapists who've attended my workshops use it as a tool at the beginning of a session. When a client is overwrought, the meditation helps to calm him so he is able to enter into meaningful work with the therapist.

People who witness the meditation are sometimes leery of trying it themselves. They lack confidence in their ability to focus. Recently, Randall, who had attended a workshop, wrote me that the next day he tried co-meditation with his partner, who was going through a difficult time. He reported that both ended the session feeling greatly relaxed and unburdened. The bonus for him is that he felt he had been present for his partner.

How do you know when a person is about to die? We can't sit with her for days on end doing co-meditation.

In my experience many people wait until they are alone to die, so it is impossible to practice co-meditation at the moment of death. When it appears that the person only has several days or hours to live, meditate with her for a time each day, or several times if you're able. Your supportive presence and compassionate intention will help the person loosen her grip on life and be ready to die when the time comes.

Making the Practice Your Own

⋄ Experiment using this practice for yourself when a difficult emotion arises.

⋄ Imagine that you are about to die. Practice letting go by breathing out the "ah" sound.

⋄ If you are a caregiver, try co-meditation with some of your patients and teach it to their family members.

■

PHOWA

It is the end of a Day of Renewal Retreat for professional caregivers. The retreatants have practiced loving-kindness for themselves during this silent day. Several have not meditated before and most have never gone a full day without speaking.

During this final period, I lead a guided phowa offered for all their patients who have died during the year. The retreatants remain silent, but there are lots of tears. The day of silence and loving-kindness has opened their hearts so that they can express their grief and loss. Everyone approaches the altar, which honors their personal spirituality. They have brought rosaries, family pictures, a gold cup, crystal angels, a stone, a shell, statues of Shiva and Kuan Yin, a cross, flowers.

Each offers incense in memory of his patients who have died and tries to visualize his grief rising and dissipating with the fragrant smoke.

For many this is the high point of the day. They have been able to express their sense of grief and loss in a safe place.

Like co-meditation, phowa also comes from the Tibetan tradition. It can be used at the moment of death to help the person let go, but I also use it as a healing visualization at funerals and bereavement groups and for those who are ill. Phowa is healing as much for the sender as for the receiver.

It is not necessary to be in the dying person's presence, so you can practice this by yourself.

Guided Meditation

For some time practice mindfulness of breathing or another meditation until your mind is clear and calm. Then visualize the person for whom you are performing phowa. See her as you wish to remember her. Imagine her lying comfortably in a lovely setting—an open meadow, at the edge of the ocean, or one of her favorite places.

Then imagine that whoever or whatever is for you the source of all goodness, love, and healing in the universe appears as a bright, clear light in the sky above your friend. It can be God, Jesus, Allah, Buddha, Cosmic Consciousness, or the Absolute. The important thing is that the source of love is embodied as an orb of bright light.

You can do the forgiveness practice for your friend.

> For all the harm I have done to others, knowingly or unknowingly, forgive me.
> For all the harm others have done to me, knowingly or unknowingly, I forgive you as much as I can.
> For all the harm I have done myself, knowingly or unknowingly, I forgive myself.

Imagine that the source of love is so touched by your friend's heartfelt remorse that rays of light enter her body.

Imagine the light entering her heart. See it suffuse her body, spreading through her torso, filling her arms and legs, entering her hands and feet, reaching her fingers and toes.

Finally, imagine it entering her head.

Your friend's body is completely filled with light, and the body fades away. Nothing remains but a body of light.

Imagine your friend's body of light rising, rising, rising toward the source of love and healing in the sky.

See your friend's body of light merge with the source of love, until nothing is left but love.

Your friend has gone home.

As you follow your breath, hold this image of your friend merged with the light of love as long as you can.

What a beautiful way to remember a person who has died. The tears that may arise during the meditation are tears of connection and healing.

Going Deeper

This seems like a beautiful practice, but I'm not sure that a person who is very religious would like it.

At first I thought about this, too. I worried that I might be forcing my own beliefs on another. Initially, I practiced phowa silently for the dying person, then I began to trust my intuition about when to use it orally. Even when it seems appropriate to the circumstances, I ask the dying if they would like me to practice with them.

I find this meditation particularly helpful with the bereaved. When I was asked to say a few words at my sister's Catholic funeral mass, I led phowa for the congregation. Many people told me later that they were moved and felt as if they were helping my sister's spirit find peace. It also improved my relations with my family. They understood that my Buddhism was not in conflict with their Catholicism.

Why is forgiveness practice included in the meditation?

Some people die suddenly and others never have a chance to acknowledge the harm they may have done during their lives. Atonement (at-one-ment) is an important element of closure. First we acknowledge our harmful actions, then we atone for them, and finally we can let them go. We are giving the dying or dead person another opportunity to let go of guilt and shame as they let go of life.

At one retreat for caregivers, a man expressed resistance to loving-kindness meditation. Anger arose again and again. He stomped around the halls during walking meditation and was restless and uncomfortable during the meditation periods. At the end of the day, I led the phowa and he burst into tears. During the closing circle he revealed that for the first time since his mother's death several years before, he was able to forgive her and wish her well. His resentful feelings about his mother and his guilt at holding on to them had been revealed by metta. Phowa had opened his heart to forgiveness. The phowa meditation is as healing for the person practicing as it is for the person receiving it.

My aunt died last year. Can I still do phowa for her?

Until we die it is impossible to know for sure what happens after death. Perhaps the essence will return to nature, or the spirit will be reborn in another body, or we may achieve nirvana, or the soul will go to heaven or hell. Perhaps when we die, that's it. You can have faith in an afterlife or not.

But why not take the opportunity to call up the memory of your aunt and wish her well? As long as you cherish her memory she'll live in some way and you will still be connected with her.

How can phowa be used as a healing visualization?

At a retreat for thirty-two women who are HIV positive, I guided the phowa in this way:

Guided Meditation

Imagine yourself lying in a meadow filled with wildflowers or on the beach or in some other favorite place that is peaceful.

The sky is filled with white, puffy clouds and there is a pleasant breeze. You can smell the aroma of flowers and hear the songs of birds.

The sun is shining brightly above you.

Imagine that whoever is the source of all love and healing in the universe is embodied in the bright sun above your head. It can be God, Jesus, Allah, or the Absolute. Just envision the healing presence of the sunlight.

Begin the forgiveness practice:

> For all the harm I have done to others, knowingly or unknowingly, forgive me.
>
> For all the harm others have done to me, knowingly or unknowingly, I forgive you as much as I can.
>
> For all the harm I have done to myself, knowingly or unknowingly, I forgive myself.

Imagine that the source of love is so touched by your heartfelt plea for forgiveness, that healing rays of light are sent down to your body.

(When guiding this meditation, pause between each phrase, so that there is enough time to visualize the light traveling through the body.)

Feel the healing light enter your heart.

Imagine the light radiating through your torso, filling your chest and stomach.

Feel the healing light move through your hips, your legs, your feet, and toes.

Feel the healing light move into your shoulders, your arms, your hands, and fingers.

Finally, feel the healing light fill your head, erasing any harmful thoughts or emotions or worry.

Imagine all negativity leaving through the tips of your fingers and the tips of your toes, so that your body feels light and relaxed.

Imagine that your body is so light that it begins to float up to the sky, higher and higher, until it merges with the sun, the embodiment of love and healing.

Imagine that you are held in the arms of love and that you are safe and protected.

And while you are following your breath, hold the image of yourself merged with the loving and healing sun.

(Several minutes of silent meditation.)

Now it's time to return to the earth. Feel yourself gently floating down, like a feather.

You are floating, down, down, through the clouds, the tops of the trees, with the birds and butterflies until you gently touch the earth.

When you open your eyes, the feeling of safety and protection and healing will stay with you.

Whenever you feel worried or tense, take a couple of deep breaths and return to the image of yourself cradled by the healing light and know that all is well.

The women at the retreat were touched by this meditation even though many were Christians, with no mystical tradition. While I was guiding, there were many sighing sounds, like "hmmm" and "ah." I believe that it was the equivalent of the "amen" heard so frequently during sermons in African-American churches.

Can this meditation really heal AIDS?

The purpose of these Buddhist healing meditations is to open our hearts and minds so that spiritual and emotional healing can occur. When we are able to feel love and compassion for ourselves, our bodies are less contracted and tense. Energy flows and space is created where healing, whether through traditional Western medicine or alternative methods, is more likely to occur. The mind is very powerful. When we believe in ourselves and others believe in us, the mind can work wonders. Meditation is only one way to reach the place where healing can occur—faith, determination, discipline, energy, attitude all enter into the equation.

RITUAL—LETTING GO OF GRIEF

The long line of people made its way over the dunes toward the shore. Laughing children stripped off their shoes and skipped, while older folks gingerly picked their way through the soft sand. Some people meandered slowly, holding hands; others strode purposefully toward the sparkling ocean. The sound of bells and wooden clappers rang out in the crisp air, heralding the procession—Ching Chong Clap! Ching Chong Clap! Ching Chong Clap!

A young boy carried the rice-paper lantern inscribed with the names of friends and relatives who had died, and approached the surfer waiting at the edge of the ocean. Taking the lantern, the surfer paddled out past the breakers and rock jetty. The crowd of onlookers watched and waited, hoping that the lantern would negotiate the current, wind, and waves to carry the spirits of the dead back home. A monk chanted:

> Vast Ocean of dazzling light
> Marked by the waves of life and death,
> The tranquil passage of great calm
> Embodies the form of new and old, coming and going.
> We devoutly aspire to true compassion
> In observing the passing of our friends and relatives.
> We sincerely offer flowers, candlelight, and incense for
>   their benefit.
> May the pure lotus bloom in eternal spring
> And may the bright sunlight of wisdom shine forever,
> Banishing the dark night of ignorance.
> Farewell!

Then the lantern was released. As it sailed off, a great shout went up from those on the shore—some waved and danced, some rang bells, some hugged, and some cried; all letting go of their grief for the moment. People took the time they needed to say farewell, lingering to watch the lantern bob and weave parallel to the shore, finally retracing their steps to the terrace behind the dunes to drink a toast to their loved ones and mingle with new and old friends. *Obon* was winding to a close.

Obon is a Japanese Buddhist festival that occurs yearly to honor family members who have died. It is colorful, fun, and uplifting; seemingly, a perfect event for Peaceful Dwelling, since our mission is to provide spiritual and emotional support to those with life-threatening illness and their caregivers. A friend offered her oceanfront home in East Hampton for the ritual and invitations were mailed, encouraging our supporters to bring guests—children were especially welcomed. Those who wished to attend were asked to send in names of friends and relatives who had died so that they could be read aloud and inscribed on a floating lantern.

I thought people would come because Obon was unusual. Who could resist the lure of an exotic Buddhist ceremony, good food and wine, and a sunny Saturday afternoon at the beach? As RSVPs dribbled in, it became clear that people wanted to honor loved ones who had died—many who could not attend sent names to be remembered; others invited friends who had recently suffered a loss.

People came because they craved a ritual for letting go. A funeral had not been enough; some other rite was necessary because letting go does not happen all at once—it is piecemeal. First the body is put into the ground or ashes scattered; then clothing is given away; perhaps the family home is sold. But when one least expects it, some event or photo or song or aroma brings back the memory of the person who died and the grief erupts again. We have to experience and embrace our grief and let it go again and again and again.

During the feast of Obon, sometimes called Feeding the Hungry Ghosts, there is an altar decorated with succulent fruits and vegetables, sweets, treats, flowers, candles, and incense to draw the spirits back home for this day of remembrance. There are little animal sculptures made from vegetables to carry the spirits home. A reindeer, horse, camel, pig, dragon, serpent, porcupine, peacock, and swan adorned our altar.

The centerpiece of the ceremony was a rice-paper lantern inscribed with the names of the dead. It rested on a circular raft and was surrounded by an ivy wreath, wild berries, and ribbons. Before the ceremony, people respectfully approached the lantern to search for the names of their loved ones.

A large gong was sounded thirty-three times to summon people to the area where the ceremony would be held. Traditional chants were adapted, abridged, and translated into English because, to my surprise, there were only a handful of American Buddhist practitioners present—the vast majority came from the Christian and Jewish faiths. It seemed to make no difference—the various traditions were woven into a tapestry of love, gratitude, and honor.

A profound silence descended as the names of the dead were read aloud, each person listening with full attention to hear the names of friends. Everyone was invited to approach the altar to offer incense in memory of the dead while we chanted. There was a brief guided meditation (phowa) to wish the spirits well, and the assembly processed to the ocean to set the lantern adrift.

At Peaceful Dwelling Project the focus had been on the dying person, on making death as full and complete as possible, and helping caregivers to support themselves and the patient during illness and death; but we had neglected the friends and family members who were left behind *after* the death. Obon had created a spirit of communion. For days afterward, people called to relate their own experiences.

One woman had a young friend who had perished early in the summer in a surfing accident. Watching our surfer paddle out past the breakers, she experienced her fear of the ocean and her anger at the loss of the boy. But when the lantern was released and the surfer returned safely, her fear and anger transformed as she relaxed into a feeling of well-being.

Many people spoke of the power of the gong to quiet their minds and hearts.

The next day the hostess received a call from a distant friend. He had had a dream the night of Obon about a mutual friend who had died (and been remembered at the festival), and in the dream he had seen a brightly colored animal—a purple dragon with red eyes, eerily recalling the figure on the altar made from a Japanese eggplant with rose-hip eyes.

Another guest noticed that at the moment the lantern was released, the flock of gulls perched on the rock jetty rose as one— like a handkerchief blown aloft by the wind. Her grief disappeared on the wind as well.

During the reception, people kept returning to the highest dune to monitor the progress of the floating lantern, its candle still flickering in the dusk as the current pulled it eastward toward Montauk Point.

How satisfying this day had been! Yet many of us think rituals are beneath us or too churchy.

All cultures and religions use ritual to mark passages in life— birth, coming of age, marriage, and death. But today in the West there are not many rituals available to us. Lately people have begun to acknowledge grief and let it go by creating their own rituals. Notice how when a public figure dies or a tragedy occurs, hundreds of strangers are moved to show respect for life and honor death by creating shrines for the dead. People bring flowers, candles, balloons, poems, and photos. Some gather to pray or cry or sing hymns. Ritual is a safe way to acknowledge the transience of our own lives and to let go of grief.

Most of us can't attend our own funerals, but Bob engineered a preview. I had met him at NYU Medical Center during his treatment for AIDS. We seemed to have a lot in common, including East Hampton, where I live and where Bob and his partner had a summer home. During that summer I visited him at the starkly modern house that his architect partner had designed. Bob liked to natter on about his garden, but eventually he'd mention his dilemma—how to let his sisters know that he had AIDS and was failing. By this time, he was blind in one eye and had been hospitalized several times for pneumonia. He had been told that he had less than a year to live.

One day Bob told me that he had begun to be filled with remorse about something he had done in his youth. During a summer vacation long ago, he and a college girlfriend had gone to Central America where her father was in charge of an archeological dig. While there, Bob had found a tiny human skull and he brought it home as a souvenir. For years he had kept it in a box, never opening it, and now, as he was nearing his own death, he felt the desire to return the skull to the earth where it belonged.

Bob felt he had committed a sacrilegious act, and the skull haunted his dreams. He asked if we could have a funeral for it before he returned to his winter home in Florida. He was happy to be involved in planning the simple ceremony. A small but deep hole was dug in his garden and in it we placed the skull in its original box wrapped in white cloth. As I recited some Buddhist prayers and sounded the bell, Bob filled in the hole and we offered incense. The next day he planted a white rosebush over the grave.

Several months after he returned to Florida, I received a copy of a codicil to his will, requesting that I bury his ashes in the East Hampton garden as we had buried the skull.

Sometimes it's not enough to mentally form the intention to let go; it's necessary to follow through with a physical gesture. At funerals we toss a spadeful of dirt on the coffin or scatter ashes into the wind or sea. When we let go of painful emotions like resentment, guilt, shame, or fear, we may have to let our whole body and mind enter the process.

The beginning of a new phase of your life can be marked by ritual as well. Mary Alice is a Catholic hospice chaplain who also practices Tibetan Buddhist meditation. After being diagnosed with breast cancer, she had undergone two surgeries but was not quite ready to enter postoperative treatment. She prayed, meditated, and took her dog on a three-thousand-mile drive in the Southwest. During that pilgrimage she was able to accept her situation and surrender. The week before her chemotherapy was to begin, she wrote:

> "On the eve before chemo begins, my hair will be shaved in a dedication ceremony to the Buddha of compassion. The ceremony will ritualize the next step—initiating me into the spiritual path that cancer patients walk—offering my sufferings for the alleviation of others who suffer breast cancer. I rejoice for the opportunity to serve and dedicate my life more sincerely."

Going Deeper

I attended the funeral of a friend who died suddenly. I never had the chance to say good-bye. How can I say farewell?

At an elaborate Buddhist funeral for a respected teacher there was a fire ceremony. Each of us was asked to write a farewell message to him. Some letters were written on beautiful paper and enclosed in decorated envelopes; others were scrawled on slips of recycled paper. To the pounding of drums and the dance of a priest wielding torches with flames made of red cloth, the messages were tossed into a burning cauldron. The farewell messages were immolated, just like the teacher's body. The smoke rose, wafting in the four directions carrying our gratitude, love, and respect towards the sky. The hundreds of people there had not been present to say good-bye at his sudden death—this was our chance for closure.

Write a farewell message to your friend and burn it, imagining the smoke carrying your words to your friend.

I had a difficult relationship with my brother. There was no time to reconcile our differences and I am not able to let go of some resentments. I want to, but don't know how.

The relationship between my father and me had also been problematical—not because of what had been said, but because of what had been left unsaid. The dearth of communication during his lifetime was mirrored on his deathbed. Intubated, face covered by the oxygen mask, he was not able to answer when I said good-bye.

Almost two years passed until I was ready to confront my feelings about him. At a retreat, it was suggested that we write a letter to someone who had died, telling him all we could not say while he had lived. Then we were to answer the letter as if we were that person. I was finally ready to do this, and I sat in my room one afternoon writing letters one after another, to my father and from him—back and forth.

I was reminded of the Zen story of a bird being hatched. The mother hen pecks at the shell, the chick taps from within. Both the pecking and the tapping are necessary for the chick to be born. Writing the letters was like that for me. They began with my anger and resentment, and then took on his perspective. Gradually my stance softened as I came to understand what his life had been like. Gradually I became him and he became me.

The final part of the exercise was to read the letters aloud while imagining my father sitting in a chair near me. When the reading was finished, I envisioned my father rising, waving good-by, and leaving. I bid farewell not only to him but to the resentment I had carried for so many years. My shell cracked and I was able to emerge, free.

Only a handful of retreatants completed the exercise. They were not ready to let go. When you are ready, write a letter to your brother and see what happens.

Do rituals have to be done in a group setting?
Private rituals can be powerful and transforming. About the time I did my vision quest, I was working on my fourth and fifth steps

in a recovery program. During the quest itself, I intended to complete the sixth and seventh steps:

Step six: We're entirely ready to have God remove all
these defects of character.
Step seven: Humbly ask Him to remove our shortcomings.

As a Buddhist, I don't have a personal god, so it was up to me to let go of the shortcomings. I had camped several feet away from a stream, and on the second morning I took a stick and scratched my shortcomings in the sand at the water's edge. My intention was to let them go. By the third morning, only faint traces remained. Wind, animal tracks, and water had washed them away. I felt cleansed and fresh.

Making the Practice Your Own

⋄ When you experience harmful emotions or self-destructive
patterns, resolve to let them go by writing them down and
burning them, burying them, or scattering the pieces like
confetti. Envision them embedded in a stone that you
can toss into the sea. As you release the token, imagine
your emotion is released as well, your heart unburdened
and free.

⋄ Create a ritual for a new beginning, and let go of the past.

⋄ On the anniversary of a loved one's death, gather some
friends and relatives to pray or meditate and share memories to celebrate her life.

⋄ After a death many of us want to get rid of everything that
reminds us of the person so that we won't feel sad. Instead,
create a shrine for the person. You can place his photo in
the shrine, along with some favorite objects and an offering, perhaps a bit of his favorite food. Each morning greet
him. Say "good night" each evening. When it feels right,
begin to remove objects until only the photo is left.

◇ If someone very close to you has died, it's okay to keep something to remind you of her. Wear her bracelet, sleep with her quilt, keep her handkerchief in your pocket. Each time you notice the object, take a couple of deep breaths and wish her well. When you're ready, put the objects away.

◇ Native Americans have a giveaway after the death of a family member. Give a token object to each person who attends the memorial service. The first memorial service I officiated at was done for Rob, a designer who had died of AIDS. Although I had visited him only twice, his partner asked me to lead the service. The house was decorated with potted phalaenopsis orchids that Rob had grown. After the service, each of us received an orchid to take home. Every year when it blooms, I'm reminded of Rob and his gentle manner.

◇ If you live in the Southwest, attend a Mexican "Day of the Dead" fiesta. Create your own altar with flowers, fruit, and photos of people who have died.

Eight

Upaya

SKILLFUL MEANS TO DEEPEN PRACTICE

■

DEVELOPING A DAILY PRACTICE

You've learned how to meditate and you're beginning to feel results already—your tension level has dropped, you are sleeping better, and petty annoyances don't bother you so much. If you're ill, you may notice that your anxiety before medical tests or procedures has lessened and some chronic pain is manageable. You may even notice that you're kinder to people, less judgmental and more forgiving. You feel more connected to the world and begin to trust that things are as they should be. Now comes the hard part, keeping your practice going and growing. Without a doubt, consistency is the most important thing when you are trying to develop a steady practice.

Practice Every Day, Even if it is Only for Five Minutes

Years ago I used to run. In the spring I would begin training for the fall New York City Marathon. I'd run short distances three times a week, long distance once a week, sprints once a week, with two rest days interspersed. Over the summer and fall, the distances became longer. Hopefully, by the day of the race I'd be in peak condition. After completing the marathon I would discontinue my running routine. When I started training again in the spring, it was as if I had never run before in my life. All the speed, stamina, and flow were gone. I had to start from scratch, huffing and puffing around the reservoir in Central Park.

Meditation practice is more like marathon training than riding a bicycle. Riding a bike comes back to you, but meditation requires the commitment and discipline of a marathon runner. When you start to feel better, the temptation to quit meditating arises—"I've got it," you think. When you hit one of life's potholes, you begin to practice again.

Trying to jump-start a meditation practice when you are in extremity is difficult. All the flow and stamina that you built up has dwindled; your concentration and focus are fuzzy. Your legs begin to hurt after even a short sitting and your mind takes longer to settle down.

You need to build a bank balance of practice to carry you through. Concentration begets serenity and a feeling of well-being; mindfulness meditations help us to be present for whatever is occurring; compassion practices help us deal with unexpected emotional and physical pain. We have a set of tools to enable us to live our lives with grace and serenity. But we must keep them sharpened. Daily practice is the answer.

Bring awareness to daily activities by creating a mantra. Before you eat a meal, take a shower, or go to bed, take several mindful breaths and say your mantra. Each night before I go to sleep, I say the following mantra, which I read in a book by Robert Aitken:

Going to bed tonight
Vowing with all beings
To calm all things
Leaving the mind clear and pure.

Following my breath helps me to fall asleep quickly.

Choose a Time of Day that is Convenient
and Meditate at the Same Time Each Day

You are building body memory. If it's 6 A.M. and you're sitting cross-legged and you hear three bells, it means meditation. Your body and mind automatically know what to do.

You may be wide awake and energetic in the morning or have trouble opening your eyes when the alarm goes off. In the evening you may nod off in front of the TV or be raring to go out on the town. Each person has a different body clock. Try to work with it, instead of against it. However, if your schedule is too hectic in the morning or you can't find a quiet, private space because of family activities, you'll have to be creative. Roz has four kids clamoring for her attention all the time; she goes into the bathroom for five minutes and locks the door.

If you drive to work, somewhere along the way park your car for five or ten minutes, preferably near a lovely setting, and meditate. It's even possible to do loving-kindness meditation while driving. When you snag a seat on a commuter bus or train, meditate for five minutes. Just lower your eyes and follow your breath. Do mindfulness meditation in which you focus on your predominant experience—ambient sounds, smells, sensations, the hindrances.

You may have to squeeze in the meditation before or after lunch. But if you can't commit to the same time each day, grab any spare minutes and meditate—standing in line at the supermarket, waiting in a doctor's office, sitting at the hairdresser's. Many activities offer opportunities for mindfulness meditation.

Once you are consistently sitting for five minutes a day, vary your practice the way I varied my marathon training. Choose to sit one or two days for ten minutes. See how it feels, and when you're ready, lengthen your daily sits. Then insert one twenty-minute period each week. For most of us, it takes that long for the chatter in our minds to quiet down and for our bodies to settle in. You can also alternate sitting and walking meditation.

When you sit down to practice, decide in advance how long you're going to sit and stay there the whole time, even if your mind is scattered. We are training the mind. When the body stays still, the mind will follow, like Mary's lamb.

You may find it distracting to peek at your watch every few seconds to see how much longer you have to sit. Set a cooking timer, a wristwatch, or for a gentler reminder, make your own meditation tape: Ring a bell three times, wait five minutes, then sound the bell twice. Simply play your tape each time you want to practice. On the same tape you can record two or three silent periods of varying lengths.

Create a Special Setting

As a child, I loved rituals. During May, Mary's month, I'd make an outdoor shrine from a shoe box covered with aluminum foil, lined with blue tissue paper. A plaster statue of the Virgin rested on a bed of absorbent cotton clouds. I made a crown of tiny artificial flowers and placed a blue votive candleholder in front of her. Each evening, to my parents' dismay, I would kneel in our small front yard in Brooklyn to recite the rosary.

Although I smile when I recall the past, I realize that the attention I lavished on my shoe box/shrine was no different from the attention I pay to my zendo now. The eighteenth-century Chinese elm altar is polished—there are always fresh flowers and candles and incense. The loving way I care for my altar reflects the respect I have for my meditation practice.

It's helpful to meditate in the same place. Most of us don't have a separate room that we can use for meditation, but it may be possible to create a special corner where you can set out your cushions or chair. Put down a scatter rug, drape a cloth on the wall, or hang a picture that has spiritual connotations for you. It can be of a deity if you have a religious affiliation or a natural scene that is uplifting. Inspiring poems or prayers or mottoes can be helpful as well.

You can set up an altar on top of a dresser or attach a small shelf to the wall. At the Day of Renewal retreats that Peaceful Dwelling offers to caregivers, participants are asked to bring objects that are important to their spirituality. The altar is filled with small statues, natural objects, personal possessions, poems, and stories. Use your imagination. On the altar you can place your mala, a feather, a pebble, a statue or photo of an inspiring figure—anything that is meaningful to you.

Make your altar as inviting as possible, so that it reminds you to meditate. Try to satisfy each of the five senses:

incense for smell
flowers for sight
a stone for touch
a piece of fruit for taste
a bell for sound

Or make offerings representing the four elements:

earth—a flower
water—a tiny cup of water
fire—a candle
air—incense

Creating a sacred space or setting up an altar reminds us that we are doing a spiritual practice. A wise person said: "Prayer is talking to God; meditation is listening to God." When we sit down to meditate we are quieting our mind so that we can listen. It doesn't matter whether you believe in a supreme being or not; the silence engendered by meditation prepares us to listen to our hearts.

The altar can grow and change as you become more appreciative of the world around you. My home altar started with a statue of Kuan-yin, the Buddhist Goddess of compassion, and I added the traditional Buddhist elements of candle, incense, and flowers. Over the years, some found objects became meaningful to me—a warbler's yellow feather, a wooden *enso* (circle, the Buddhist symbol of oneness) carved by a departed friend, the silver plastic letters *RA* from my medicine walk, tiny Mexican Day of the Dead musicians.

At Christmas time I also set up a traditional crèche. One Buddhist teacher has a large rock on the altar, but no statue. Everything is sacred, we just haven't realized it yet. As your realization grows, so will your altar.

If you arrange an altar, you might decide to go through a ritual before you meditate. I make a standing bow in front of the altar and light the candle and incense. You too may wish to light a candle or incense or make a bow. Do whatever feels right to you. Sometimes, during the day I catch a glimpse of the altar and light some incense; it brings me back to the present moment and helps center me.

Your special place can be outdoors. A friend, Millicent, has placed a chair next to a wild holly tree in her yard—this is where she meditates, weather permitting. Another friend likes to walk on the beach—this is her cathedral.

If you don't have room to set up a permanent altar, create an altar in a box, somewhat like my shoe box/shrine. Several artists have created elaborate boxes. Look at the work of Joseph Cornell or Louise Nevelson for ideas. Setting up an altar or shrine reminds us that we are doing a spiritual practice. Its presence reminds us to *do* the practice.

Find Support for your Practice

The Buddha said, "Having excellent friends is not half the practice, it is the entire practice."

Although there are ancient stories of monks retreating to caves or huts for many years to practice in seclusion, most of us don't have that opportunity or the discipline to follow through.

It is difficult enough for us to commit to getting up fifteen minutes earlier each day to meditate. There's always something to interfere—sleepiness, an early business appointment, getting the kids ready for school. Sometimes our families don't understand what we're doing and they create impediments to our practice. It's important to find a *sangha* (group dedicated to practice) to meditate with.

Try to locate a sitting group in your community. Even if they are not practicing the same way you are, it's helpful to check in periodically with others who meditate. The group energy will sustain you and you'll be able to sit for a longer period of time.

If you cannot find a congenial group, start your own. Putting up a notice in a bookstore or at a college is one way of attracting like-minded people, or place an ad in the local free newspaper. If you belong to a support group or attend exercise class, approach other members about forming a sitting group. Even two or three people sitting together once a week create a supportive atmosphere. Find a spiritual book that you like and discuss it with the group.

Whether you are sitting alone or with a group, you can deepen your practice by attending a one-day, weekend, or week-long retreat or workshop—check out the Web, bulletin boards at local bookstores, or the resource list at the back of this book. Attending a retreat will also give you the opportunity to talk with a spiritual teacher who may give you advice about your practice.

I was blessed when I decided to practice seriously; there was a Zen master less than ten miles from my home. You may have more difficulty finding a spiritual mentor, but it's possible. Mention to as many people as you can that you are looking for a teacher; there may be one near you. If not, see the resource list for titles of magazines that specialize in meditation—many have listings of centers that publish newsletters and audio and videocassettes. Be sure to look on the Internet, because some centers have Web sites that publish a teacher's talks or allow you to ask questions.

When you begin it's fine to check out different teachers until you find one that is compatible. After you've made your decision, stay with that teacher for a reasonable length of time. It's helpful to work with one person who knows you and your practice well, rather than to flit from flower to flower.

In ancient times when someone wanted to begin a spiritual practice, he abandoned his home, family, and work to set off on foot to find a teacher. Today, not many of us are willing to go this far. So we rely on books, magazines, the Internet, and word of mouth; the teaching comes to us. All we have to do is take advantage of it. All we have to do is practice.

Ultimately the responsibility is ours. The Buddha said, "Don't believe my words, find out for yourself." Practice is the way to find wisdom and compassion. It reveals our innate loving-kindness and equanimity and frees us from self-centered desires.

How do you get to this place of freedom? Practice.

Resources

■

MINDFULNESS

Gass, Robert. *Chanting: Discovering Spirit in Sound*. New York: Broadway Books, 1999.

Kabat-Zinn, Jon. *Wherever You Go, There You Are*. New York: Hyperion, 1994.

Rosenberg, Larry. *Breath by Breath*. Boston: Shambala, 1998.

Thich Nhat Hanh. *The Blooming of a Lotus: Guided Meditations for Healing and Transformation*. Boston: Beacon, 1993.

Thich Nhat Hanh. *A Guide to Walking Meditation*. Nyack, NY: Fellowship Publications, 1985.

■

METTA AND THE BRAHMA VIHARAS

Salzberg, Sharon. *Lovingkindness: The Revolutionary Art of Happiness*. Boston: Shambala, 1995.

Bastis, Madeline. *Metta: Open Your Heart to Love and Compassion for Yourself and Others*. (audio-cassette) East Hampton: Peaceful Dwelling, 1996.

■

TONGLEN

Chödrön, Pema. *The Wisdom of No Escape*. Boston: Shambala, 1991.

Chödrön, Pema. *When Things Fall Apart*. Boston: Shambala, 1998.

■

LETTING GO
(PHOWA AND CO-MEDITATION)

Boerstler, Richard W. *Letting Go: A Holistic and Meditative Approach to Living and Dying*. South Yarmouth, MA: Associates in Thanatology, 1991.

Sogyal Rinpoche. *The Tibetan Book of Living and Dying*. San Francisco: HarperSanFrancisco, 1992.

■

FINDING A MEDITATION CENTER
AND RETREATS

Lorie, Peter, and Julie Foakes. *The Buddhist Directory*. Boston: Tuttle Publishing, 1997.

Morreale, Don. *The Complete Guide to Buddhist America*. Boston: Shambala, 1998.

■

MAGAZINES

Inquiring Mind. (published semi-annually)
Shambala Sun. (published bi-monthly)
Tricycle: the Buddhist Review. (published quarterly)

ABOUT PEACEFUL DWELLING PROJECT—
"THE RETREAT WITHOUT WALLS"

Peaceful Dwelling Project is a not-for-profit educational organization that promotes the use of meditation for spiritual, emotional, and physical healing by offering retreats, workshops, classes, lectures, and publications for people with life-challenging illness, healthcare professionals, clergy from different traditions, and all who wish to learn meditation.

As yet, Peaceful Dwelling does not have its own residential center, but rents facilities to present workshops and retreats. Peaceful Dwelling Project can facilitate a workshop or retreat at your location. For more information contact:

Peaceful Dwelling Project
2 Harbourview Drive
East Hampton, NY 11937-1766
Phone: 631–324–3736
Fax: 631–324–5353
E-mail: info@peacefuldwelling.org
Web site: www.peacefuldwelling.org